Growing Hope

GROWING HOPE

*Sowing Seeds of Positive Change
in Yourself and the World*

SUE PATTON THOELE

CONARI PRESS

First published in 2004 by Conari Press,
an imprint of Red Wheel/Weiser, LLC
York Beach, ME
With offices at:
368 Congress Street
Boston, MA 02210
www.redwheelweiser.com
Copyright © 2004 Sue Patton Thoele

Prayer for Protection by James Dillet Freeman used with permission of Unity, publisher.

Library of Congress Cataloging-in-Publication Data
Thoele, Sue Patton.
  Growing hope : sowing seeds of positive change in yourself and the world / Sue Patton Thoele.
      p. cm.
  ISBN 1-57324-911-4
  1. Hope. I. Title.
  BF575.H56T48 2004
  170'.44—dc22

                                            2003018339

Typeset in Weiss and Charlotte Sans
Printed in the United States
RRD
11 10 09 08 07 06 05 04
 8 7 6 5 4 3 2 1

To those who
      carry a commitment
            to wholeness
In the midst of
      chaos
            acrimony
                  and ignorance,
Thank you. . . .

To those who
      fan the embers
            of compassion
With unwavering
      acceptance
            inclusion
                  and service,
Thank you. . . .

You are the
      Light Bearers.
You are our
      Hope. . . .

CONTENTS

Acknowledgments

The creation of a book is a partnership between many people. I am incredibly blessed by the quality and compassion of the partners who have helped me bring *Growing Hope* to fruition.

A thousand thank you's to:

Jan Johnson, Publisher and brilliant woman, with whom the idea of growing hope first came to light.

Caroline Pincus, Book Midwife and editor extraordinaire, who deftly and gently turned my breech manuscript around and helped birth it painlessly.

The Red Wheel/Conari women: Jill Rogers, Robyn Heisey Rowe, Lucine Kasbarian, Laura Lee Mattingly, Kathleen Wilson Fivel, Liz Wood, Kate Hartke, Jennifer Brown, and Emily Sauber for their wonderful attitudes and all around helpfulness.

Pam Suwinsky, Copy Editor, who deserves all the credit for the spit 'n' polished final edition.

Brenda Knight, Idea Mistress and Sales Whiz, who is a continuing inspiration and energizer.

Michael Kerber, President of Red Wheel / Weiser / Conari Press, who is an efficient and compassionate businessman.

The unseen, ever present, and eternally appreciated helpers without whom I could not do this work.

Judith Mangus, Mugs Holifield, and Mary Banks, soul sisters, who are unfailingly encouraging and incredibly patient with my periodic whining.

Annabelle Woodard—Spiritual Mother, Mentor, Experiential Mystic, and dear Friend—who is Magic in a wonderfully human way.

Mike, Brett, Paige, Lynnie, Josh, Alex, Grant, Shawn, Chad, and Caitlin who teach me about love, laughter, and letting go.

And, of course, Gene Thoele—partner, lover, friend, and clown—who steadfastly makes our life safe, secure, and laughter-filled.

CHAPTER 1

GROWING HOPE

Hope is the
> sweet dove
>> of peace

Whose wings restart
My heart
> when it falters.

—AUTHOR

Hope is in short supply these days. We look around and don't necessarily see a lot to be hopeful *about*. But the truth is, each of us carries within our hearts the seeds of enduring hope. Growing hope is an inside job. And like anything worth cultivating—happiness, success, peace of mind, a loving family—hope requires conscious effort and committed action to be able to grow deep roots in our heart and soul. Even the most resilient seeds can fail to sprout when buried in the harsh soil of pain and fear. But I've found that with love, intention, and a little help, we all have the ability to create a fertile field within us where hope can grow, flourish, and eventually spread outward to inspire and uplift others. Happiness, serenity, and circumstances can help bolster our feelings of hope, but they don't *create* them. *We* do. I can just hear some of you murmuring, "Bummer."

I know, because I fell into a self-dug pit of hopelessness when first contemplating writing this book. Nagging internal voices filled me with doubt: "What a huge and important subject. What can *I* possibly say that would help?" "No matter what I write, it will be a mere drop in the bucket. . . ."

Stymied, I began consciously *courting* hope by practicing many of the ideas, attitudes, and activities I planned to incorporate into the book if and when I ever managed to start writing it! To get myself started, each morning I would look in the mirror and assure myself, "You can do this. You don't have to go it alone. . . . Relax and let whatever needs to be said come through." I also devised a simple ritual to do before sitting down at the computer. I invited my angels and muse to be with me and asked for my little self to get out of the way so that my higher Self—or God's energy—could flow through me to be of service.

Thankfully, hope eventually took root, and inspiration and excitement began to replace fear and lack of confidence. Probably the greatest boost I received came from a Gandhi quote I "accidentally" found:

> Almost anything you do seems insignificant. It is very important that you do it. You must be the change you wish to see in the world.

And that's it, in a nutshell, isn't it? We need to create, within ourselves, the changes for which we yearn.

If we want a world filled with hope and kindness, a world lopsided toward love, we need to cultivate and nurture those qualities within ourselves.

Why the Erosion of Hope?

Those who are animated by hope can perform what would seem impossibilities to those who are under the depressing influence of fear.
—RACHEL ROBARDS JACKSON

So many people these days have the feeling that an apocalypse of one sort or another is marching up their

3

front steps, about to knock on—or *in*—their door. It's tempting to belabor the difficulties in our world (personal and collective) and to berate those we think are responsible, including ourselves. However, I am convinced that both of these actions are detrimental to our sense of well-being and inevitably lead to a more profound loss of hope. No, instead of dwelling on the negative, we have to work at accentuating the positive.

That doesn't mean we can totally eliminate what we experience as negative. Of course we can't. But before we can begin to emphasize the positive we have to better understand what's driving the erosion of hope and the growth of despair. I see four factors:

1. *Personal Pain*

Although some of us retain our sense of hope no matter what happens and seem to glide through personal setbacks and tragedies as gracefully as professional ice skaters, many of us find personal pain depressing, even debilitating. If you fall in the latter category, please know that psychology and medical science are proving that becoming depressed by pain isn't a sign of flawed character or wimpy constitution; it is a matter of undisciplined thought processes, aggravated by variations in our fundamental chemical and physical makeup. On the

4

flip side, the sister discovery is that *we can alter our natural inclinations* and learn coping and thriving skills that can lead to peace of mind, personal fulfillment, and increased happiness.

With this in mind, I wrote *Growing Hope*—to help you make a friend of your mind, create constructive responses to stress, and strengthen your resilience, while continuing to honor your innate sensitivity. I know these ideas work, because by using them I've surrendered my title of Grand Duchess of Worry and Impatience (my mother was the Exalted Empress) and become only an occasional visitor to Impatient Worryland. And what a relief it is.

Renewing hope and regaining a sense of balance and rightness within yourself may not be easy tasks—indeed they are not—but they *are* simple. As spring trees and flowers teach us, the ability to bloom anew is always present. And it brings incredible rewards both to you and to those you love.

2. *Media Mayhem and Madness*

Recently, my son did a swim-with-sharks scuba dive. As you can imagine, it was not a trip my mother-self heartily endorsed. He told me it was perfectly safe because the vast majority of the sharks ignore the insignificant little humans in the water and zero in on

5

the dead, bloody stuff called chum that the dive guides spread in the water. The resemblance to the media with its penchant for emphasizing violence is hard to miss.

In a review of Michael Moore's movie *Bowling for Columbine*, Robert W. Butler of the *Kansas City Star* pondered the culpability of the media in America's love affair with guns and violence when he wrote, "What is the role of the American media, powered by the voracious monster of 24-hour cable news? Why is it that coverage of violent crime has soared 600 percent even as homicides have fallen 20 percent?" From watching and reading the news, who would have guessed that homicides have fallen 20 percent? No one. How could we, given the media's penchant for embracing the "If it bleeds, it leads" standard?

The way I see it, if hope is a helium balloon, society, through its cohort the media, has a thousand pins at the ready to prick it full of holes. While it's important to know pertinent news, our hope and optimism flag when fed a steady diet of the bad, ugly, and violent. It's best to choose to grab the information we need, then turn off and tune out.

3. *Economic Iffiness*

The other day I overheard a woman at the grocery store saying, with a rueful chuckle, "My 401K is *not* okay!" She is not alone. I am not very financially savvy, but it appears as if the economy in general and the stock market in particular have been struck by something akin to perpetual PMS. Because of the insecurity created by this malaise, many of us are experiencing, firsthand, a sense of economic vulnerability that we've only heard about in discussions regarding the Great Depression.

No longer able to hang our hopes on external financial circumstance, we would be wise to *plan* for the future but not live in *fear* of it. Accomplishing that Herculean feat requires that we develop an ability to nullify fear and create a sustainable, inner sanctuary of peace and positivism.

4. *Sandpapered Senses*

The effects of personal pain, media madness, and an iffy economy on our sense of hope are readily apparent. Less obvious, but no less draining, is the bombardment of unrelenting stimuli hailing on us wherever we turn. Babies know their limits and, when overstimulated, are not at all shy about sharing them with whoever is available. We recognize the signs in little ones and act in their best interest by removing them from chaos, comforting them with rocking and crooning, and, best of all, encouraging them to nap. Few of us adults are as consciously aware of our own needs. The omnipresence of loud music, cell phone shouting, loss of personal space, miles-long to-do lists, the assault of sugar and caffeine, and our own internal demands for performance and personal perfection have caused us to lose track of our own saturation points. Not honoring our sensory and emotional limits is causing us to "numb out" and anesthetize ourselves before we blow a fuse and strike out or stroke out from an overload of energy.

When we're at the mercy of overwhelming stimuli, none of us has the ability to tap into our well of inherent hope. In fact, instead of taking gentle care of ourselves when signs of overstimulation surface, we often push ourselves harder and castigate ourselves about our imagined failings. I know, because that's exactly what I used to do to myself.

Until a few years ago, I was ashamed of the "oversensitive" label some significant others had given me, and as a result, I added a few equally unflattering labels of my own. I thought I "should" be able to tolerate the involuntary auditory assault of loud music at home and in public places and chastised myself for the "bitchiness" that arose when I said Yes too often, didn't get time alone, and ground my teeth to the bone when people chewed loudly. Sandpapered senses were a huge factor in my own erosion of hope—and still are, when I don't pay attention.

Luckily, a friend introduced me to a book that has been a real lifesaver for me. It is entitled *The Highly Sensitive Person: How to Survive When the World Overwhelms You* by Elaine Aron. According to Dr. Aron, if you tend to feel that the world around you—and usually within as well—accosts you with too much, too often, too loud, and too long, you are probably an HSP (Highly Sensitive Person) and need to accept that your personal wiring can assimilate less stimulation than is usually present in your life. I took three important pointers from Aron's book: First, I've been able let go of the unflattering and untrue labels that others and I had given me. Second, knowing that I'm simply wired differently from about 75 percent of the other people, I now either make sure to take care of myself when going into a situation ripe for overload or try to avoid those situations for which there are no good solutions. Third, my husband now understands that my wants and needs are not unreasonable and accepts me as I am. All of those adjustments have made a huge difference in my life and help me maintain an attitude of hope and a healthy lifestyle.

Many of the suggestions and ideas in *Growing Hope* are intended to help you remove as much of the sandpaper stimuli from your life as you can so that you have more energy for planting and harvesting seeds of hope and creativity.

Consciously Courting Hope

I know that we are in hellish times but that the world is rich in peace and mercy and beauty.
—ANNE LAMOTT

For many years I volunteered my services as a therapist, chaplain, and bereavement group leader at hospice. The main regret I heard from both patients and bereaved persons was some version of, "I wish I'd been more aware of what I really wanted. . . . I wish I'd paid more attention to those I love. . . . I wish I'd lived *my* life rather than the one I thought was expected of me." In other words, at the end of life, many people wished they had been more conscious about important aspects of their lives and relationships. Instead, many felt that they'd been swept along by external currents as easily as a leaf is swept downstream, and sorely regretted having lived by rote rather than by choice and design. One woman's statement was particularly poignant. Holding my hand, Hilda whispered, "I'm dying before I've really been happy or ever been really myself."

In my heart, I often thank Hilda for reminding me to remain conscious, choose to be me, and choose to be happy. Of course, no one feels Pollyanna-happy all the time, but we can learn to make conscious choices that invite peace, harmony, and hope into our hearts and souls a majority of the time. To the well-known adage, "Anything worth doing is worth doing right," I would add, "Anything worth doing is worth doing *consciously*."

You may be wondering if we even have the right to grow hope and choose happiness when there is so much pain in the world. I suggest that it is precisely *because* there is so much pain in the world that we must grow hope and choose happiness. One of the most powerful ways we can affect the larger whole and help create peace is through generating positive feelings and attitudes and bringing light into the darkness within and without. Peace on earth begins within individual hearts.

Finding Balance and Ballast

Everything starts with awareness. Take a moment to think about what and who may be getting shortchanged in your life. What might you wish to do differently to attain day-to-day equilibrium? For me, the answer is usually much the same: Paint, meditate, and exercise more regularly. Both painting and meditating clear the clutter from my mind, and exercise cleanses my body and emotions, which is very balancing. Gretchen, a client of mine, had a different answer: "Work less, worry less, and be less uptight." Without a moment's hesitation, another friend replied, "Oh, that's easy! I'd be a lot more balanced if I lived more in faith and less in fear." I bet hers is a pretty good answer for most of us. I know it is for me.

You will do yourself, your health, and your relationships
a loving service when you have the courage to gently explore
the imbalances in your life and take steps to correct them.

Once we become aware of what needs rebalancing and begin to work toward achieving more symmetry, it's immensely helpful to know what types of ballast keep us on an even keel. Friendships, creative outlets, playing sports, being with our children, taking time for ourselves—there are so many. My favorite *Webster's* definition of *ballast* is "something that gives stability or weight especially in character, conduct, ideas, or morals." The vast majority of individuals whom I interviewed for *Growing Hope* felt that a belief in something greater than themselves bolstered their spirits and kept them afloat. Many mentioned that the love and support of family and friends sustained them during stormy times, and almost everyone agreed that being able to help others gave them a sense of meaning and purpose that was instrumental in their being able to "keep on keepin' on" when the going got tough. It appears that ballast often incorporates faith, love, and service. Those seem to be pretty good indicators of stability in character, conduct, and morals, don't they?

Right now, ask yourself, What keeps me afloat? What acts as a life jacket or compass for me during turbulent and stressful times?

Groundswell of Hope

I received a most welcome and unexpected bit of ballast as I was researching this book. I became aware of a growing global effort among conscious and concerned people to encourage hope in themselves and others, even in the face of seemingly hopeless circumstances. Though they may not even know of each other, together they are creating a groundswell of hope in the world.

One such effort is a new magazine entitled, simply, *Hope.* The sample issue I received was filled with uplifting articles and suggestions about how individuals could regain and pass on hope. Another unexpected emissary for hope was a recent *Time* magazine Special Issue focusing on "How Your Mind Can Heal Your Body." An article I especially enjoyed was titled "Say 'Om'

Before Surgery." It was written by cardiovascular surgeon Mehmet Oz and stressed how his patients at Columbia Presbyterian Medical Center in New York City responded much better to surgery and recovered more quickly and completely when they were taught to meditate, let go of anxiety, and hold onto hope. At the end of the article Dr. Oz wrote, "Conventional medicine will keep breaking new ground in treatment and prevention, yet often the most effective solutions are found in the medicine cabinet of the mind. In one study, meditating 15 minutes twice daily reduced physician visits over a six month period and saved the healthcare system $200 a patient. Sometimes the best things in life are free."

I love that: the medicine cabinet of the mind.

In my town alone I know of several groups who are meeting to meditate on peace and to talk about ways in which the members can foster a sense of brother- and sisterhood within our community. One group's focus is to pray for world leaders and visualize them filled with compassion, a desire to understand their people, and a willingness to look beyond their own egos and the politics of their countries in order to foster goodwill and fairness in their country and beyond. My women's group (of just four members) spends 10 minutes visualizing feminine energy flooding our planet for an infusion of compassion, inclusion, and connection. That may all sound impossibly optimistic, but every wonderful reality was once a dream most people would have considered farfetched and unattainable. I, for one, am tremendously grateful to the conscientious and hope-filled people who are sending prayers and energy toward the evolution of a greater good for all.

We need to do everything in our power to keep the groundswell going and growing. We owe it not only to ourselves but especially to our children. As Maya Angelou wrote, "Surviving is important, but thriving is elegant." It is our responsibility to consciously court hope as an integral part of thriving and to pass that ability on to our children.

Personal Oases

We can't grow hope in depleted soil. Exhaustion, overwhelm, and the anxiety that comes from feeling spread too thin almost always obliterate hope from our emotional screens. That's why it's so important to find ways to renew and restore our inner resources. We need to give ourselves permission to find personal and familial oases—those places and activities that provide refuge and sanctuary from feelings of overwhelm and allow us to rest and regroup. Our oases not only help revive our energy, they can also be havens of fun, intimacy,

15

and meaning. Then, rested and restored, we can give hope roots in the deep soils of inner security rather than in the sandy and shallow soils of external circumstances.

David, a minister I spoke with, said that his spiritual thirst for meaning—especially when he is downhearted and questioning God—is best quenched through activism of almost any kind. He serves meals to the homeless, gathers food and goods for those in need, and counsels people struggling with difficulties. David's oasis is outward service augmented by inner prayer.

Your oasis may be exactly the opposite. You may need to back away from giving for a while and do something for you and you alone, something that makes your heart sing. In fact, singing is an oasis for Marion, one of my clients. Although an agnostic in theory, she gains much joy and meaning from singing sacred music with a large choir. She absolutely radiates euphoria after concerts. "It's what keeps me grounded and sane," Marion exclaims.

My husband, Gene, and I create mini-oases when one or more of our grandsons comes to visit. Although keeping up with toddlers is neither quiet nor serene, their innocence and authenticity bring ballast to our lives and fill our hearts to overflowing.

Extroverts may find a crowded sports bar very relaxing and rejuvenating, while an introvert's idea of heaven may be sitting in silence hand-stitching a quilt or knitting an afghan. Some of us calm ourselves through a combination of out-there and in-there activities. It doesn't matter a hoot what kind of oasis you choose, as long as it brings you the balance and ballast for which you are yearning at the time.

Probably the most reliable oasis we can find is as close as our own heartbeat. I'm talking about the value of simply turning your attention to your heart. You may be skeptical. I certainly was. But, the first time I purposely put my hands over my heart, thanked it for serving me so faithfully, and then simply continued to rest for a few moments in awareness of my heart, I couldn't stop the tears from sliding down my cheeks. They seemed to be tears of recognition and gratitude rather than of sadness or unresolved pain.

There are no *shoulds* or *have to's* connected to seeking the sanctuary of our heart oasis. Simply turning your attention to your heart, in whatever ways feel right to you, consciously courts hope and its cousins, relaxation and calmness.

Hope is a matter of heart.

A PRACTICE
FOR GROWING HOPE IN YOUR HEART

Take a moment now and focus on your heart, allowing yourself to sink into and absorb the love that naturally emanates from it. In the theater of your mind, visualize your heart energy. What color is it? How does it feel: warm, cool, soft, breezy . . . ? Talk to your heart even if you feel silly doing so. Thank it for all it does for you, and ask what it would like you to do for yourself and the greater good. Pay attention, and accept any insights or feelings that come. Or don't come. Simply hanging out with your heart provides a wonderful and potentially healing oasis. Try this exercise whenever you're feeling devoid of hope.

As with anything that grows, hope needs conscious care and compassionate attention in order to bloom. As hope takes root and flowers, we will be well equipped to maintain emotional and spiritual balance and harmony during both calm and confusing times.

CHAPTER 2

SOWING HOPE

Hope waits patiently in

the ground of our being

Knowing she will

eventually bloom anew

in our hearts.

Hope, as the saying promises,

does spring eternal.

—AUTHOR

Sometimes, especially during and after an emotional drought or a flood of difficulties, we need to reseed our internal gardens. Just as Mother Nature continually replenishes her plants by blowing seeds and pods to their new homes, we need to sow new seeds of hope. While we take it for granted that nature needs reseeding and understand that it's important to replace the flora and fauna in our stomachs after taking antibiotics, it's equally important to accept that our own soul gardens need reseeding, too.

I don't know about you, but it helps me to know that this is natural and normal. Then I'm able to stop resisting and get the energy I need to start doing what needs to be done.

The first step is simply to accept the fact that we need to *help* hope bloom in our hearts.

An attitude of hope is one of the cornerstones for a meaningful and joyous life.

Regaining Inherent Hope

Hope is the feeling you have that
the feeling you have isn't permanent.
—JEAN KERR

I like to say that hope is more like a potato than a tomato. Tomatoes grow in plain sight and can be picked right off the vine, but we need to dig in the dirt to find potatoes. The same is true of hope. Sometimes we simply have to muck around in our inner dirt a little in order to find seeds of hope. But, no matter how deeply buried or how tough the excavation, hope is always there somewhere. It's inherent within us. So, no matter how overgrown and obscured by loss and pain the path to hope may be, we can find it again.

Drinking from the Well

In a desire to understand how to rediscover our sometimes elusive internal wellspring of hope, I asked a number of friends, clients, family members, and acquaintances, "How do you keep hope alive in your soul?" Some of their answers follow:

- Believe in a Higher Power that doesn't need to get elected.
- Consciously try to stay out of the fear energy that is prevalent in the media and society at large.
- Trust in my relationship with God.
- Believe that, in the grand scheme of things, we're taken care of no matter how dire external circumstances appear.
- Ask people who love me to remind me that I'm loveable. And tell me why.
- Be aware of and grateful for all my current blessings.

- Stay connected with the spiritual source that feeds me at the time.
- Read and hear uplifting stories.
- Do something loving for a family member, friend, or maybe even a stranger or myself.

I was struck by the fact that all of their answers indicated an underlying spiritual belief, so I asked the same question of people whom I knew to be unsure about religion or spirituality. Their answers:

- Be kind and gentle with myself, especially when I'm vulnerable.
- Turn to friends and family for support and reassurance.
- Become especially aware of signs of hope such as the stars, sun, and Earth that all keep doing their thing no matter what we humans do. I trust the "Honorable Universe" when I can't believe in the "Honorable Human."
- Do something for those less fortunate.
- Take care of my body. . . . Keep it healthy and rested.
- Play with my baby and drink in her innocence and natural goodness.
- First I complain and whine, and then I turn

my attention to the good stuff in my life, and in the world. It's there, but you have to look for it and focus on it.

Take a moment to ask yourself, How do I keep hope alive in my soul?

It's worth noting that no one in either group balked at the word *soul* in the question. In fact, all their answers touched on heart qualities such as love, support, connection, service, creativity, self-care, positive focus, and gratitude. As mystics, poets, and spiritual teachers have long believed, the heart is the seat of the soul.

From my personal and professional experience, I have observed that it takes a belief in and reliance on something higher, deeper, wider, and richer than ourselves to grow hope. It's no accident that the third step in all Twelve-Step programs is "We made a decision to turn our will and our lives over to the care of God as we understood Him."

As the sage Rabindranath Tagore wrote, "Faith is the bird that feels the light and sings when the dawn is still dark." When David, my minister friend, is in the metaphorical belly of the whale, as Jonah was, it eventually dawns on him that he needs to remember what he's forgotten: God watches his back. As a result, consciously or subconsciously, he turns toward God and begins to see the light even before it appears. If a man

who has chosen a career based on spirituality struggles with personal darkness and emerges once again
into the light of faith and hope, I trust that you and I
can drink from that well also, even while darkness seems
to reign.

Hope and Expectation

It's important to distinguish between hope and expectation. Hope is about looking for the good and believing it will come; *expectation*, on the other hand, has
certain outcomes in mind. For instance, I hope that I
find the strength and courage to grow through the
challenge of a cancer diagnosis. On the other hand, I
might expect that doing a certain medical procedure
will cure me. My expectation is fulfilled only if I continue to live free from cancer. Cured or not, however,
my hope of strength, courage, and growth can come
true.

As a parent, I hope and pray I am able to do my best
and that my children *will* become happy, well-adjusted,
caring adults. I can also expect that if I do my best, my
children will become wonderful people and think I'm
fabulous, to boot. My hope keeps me doing my best;
my expectation sets me up for frustration or failure. In
both the cancer and the parenting scenarios, there are
simply too many variables at work to guarantee that

my expectations will be met. Expectation often becomes a quagmire of disappointment, while the effervescence of hope allows our spirits to soar.

Recently a young woman whom I consider a chosen daughter gave me a bumper sticker that says, "Something wonderful is about to happen." My heart immediately responded, *Yes!* Dyed-in-the-wool optimists having a difficult time would probably add, "Something wonderful—or at least growth producing—will eventually come out of the darkness and difficulties I'm experiencing now." That's hope in all its glory.

Three years ago, my friend Kate died of ovarian cancer at age fifty-seven. After hearing the latest in her physical treatments and symptoms, I always asked her the same question: "And how is your heart?" While she could still speak, her answer was always the same: "My heart is good. My heart is always good." What a wonderful teacher she was to me. As a therapist, I've seen countless clients respond to adversity in much the same way Kate did. In fact, most of us can probably remember a time when we sprang back to life even though our wellspring of hope seemed parched and barren and we had to dig in the dirt to find and clear it. That's how hope works. It's there all the time, just waiting to be set free.

Embracing and Transforming Pain

The way toward freedom from a situation
often lies in acceptance of the situation.
—RACHEL NAOMI REMEN

We can't sow hope in frozen ground.

This lesson, like so many in life, kept showing up for me until I really got it.

I don't think I was actually taught to run from and resist pain at all costs. Nonetheless, I carried the run-and-resist habit from childhood well into adulthood. Avoidance seemed to be working moderately well until my first husband left me and I became a single mom with two little boys. Unable to ignore the pain and shame of divorce and the trepidation of single parenthood, I searched for ways to bring meaning to the experience and hope back to my soul. Much to my surprise, many teachers and sages I came to admire advised *embracing* pain rather than avoiding it. Stoically enduring unavoidable suffering I could understand, but embracing pain? No way.

Finally, through hospice work and my private counseling practice—and of course the ever-present personal work—I came to accept that embracing pain leads to its transformation. Resisting pain not only doesn't make it go away, it actually magnifies it. Believing in the wisdom of embracing pain doesn't, as my spiritual mother Annabelle would say, "automagically" make it easy to do. We need continually to remind ourselves not to close down, clam up, and tough out pain alone, especially not emotional pain such as depression and hopelessness.

Nobel Peace Prize-nominee Thich Nhat Hanh encourages us to *recognize a painful feeling, smile at it, and bring it relief by embracing it tenderly like a mother.* Ironically, as I write this, I am filled with pain concerning one of my children. While lying sleepless and sad, I visualized angels surrounding my child and also asked for my special angel to help me cradle my mother's heart. In my mind's eye, I imagined the angel tenderly holding my child, myself, and my heart as a warm light flowed softly around us all. Nothing dramatic happened, but I did fall asleep soon after.

Perhaps the simple act of opening up to my feelings and asking for help embracing them comforted me enough to quiet my mind and allow sleep to work its magic. In order to heal into inherent hopefulness, it's so important we become a loving mother to ourselves and learn to kiss our own owies with care and gentleness.

Thich Nhat Hanh expands on the benefits of embracing pain: *Embrace your suffering, and let it reveal to you the way to peace.* This holy man's prescription seemed especially helpful for my hospice patients. Many whose hope had been snuffed out by fear—fear that they couldn't endure the pain, were surely headed to hell, had not done enough or been good enough, or that their children would flounder without them—found peace and hope by embracing the very fears that had tormented them. Those who accepted and embraced their pain and grief—no matter what form it took—often became serene and hopeful about their situations and very compassionate toward others, which brought great comfort to their families.

Because painful feelings are emotional bullies fueled by fear, the best way to transform them is to face them head-on.

In the throes of a bout of righteous resistance to letting go of what I perceived to be an unkind and undeserved emotional attack, I wrote the following two ditties:

Resist, resist, resist . . .
glimmers of possible surrender . . .
No way!
resist, resist, resist . . .
More persistent thoughts of surrender . . .
I can't! I won't! I'm right!

> resist, resist, resist . . .
> Maybe I can surrender—a little . . .
> resist, resist, resist. . . .

and

> Shredded, bleeding, broken
> Hopeless
> Maybe I'll at least be
> good compost
> For those who follow!

Writing these poems gave me an inescapable peek at how much my Drama Queen personality was enjoying being wronged. In her element at center stage, she was tearing garments and crying copious tears. Writing gave her a chance to express herself and me a chance to temper her behavior and chuckle at myself in the process.

Fight, Flight, Freeze, or Face?

Many of us have experienced times when we've been frozen in place, either physically or emotionally, by a difficult personal confrontation. I can fight with the best of 'em when it comes to physical danger or acting in an emergency, but only recently have I been able to stop freezing when someone confronts me directly about something emotional. Why? Because confrontation scared me silly, and the fear froze my mind, numbed my self-esteem, and shook my whole body. Response of any kind was impossible as long as I was enveloped in fear.

I've worked long and hard on learning to face the core fears and beliefs responsible for my tendency to freeze when I think I'm being emotionally attacked. Or, I sigh to admit, even vaguely criticized. I'd have to say fear of rejection is my biggest bugaboo. If someone speaks harshly or unfairly to me, the response "I must be a bad person" is almost Pavlovian.

A friend of mine says that fear is a gut-jerk reaction. Most of us emerge from childhood with gut-jerk reactions to some circumstances and experiences. While the familiar gut-jerk response may continue to be our first reaction—our default setting, if you will—one of the major tasks of adulthood is learning to neutralize these subconscious reactions and behaviors and *choose* more appropriate ones. In other words, we may still react with the fear, but we are able to regroup quickly and respond more appropriately.

My determination to face and embrace my fear of rejection seems to be paying off. Just the other day I was able to calmly and rationally respond to an undeserved emotional barrage from someone I love dearly. Granted, my stomach was doing gymnastics, but neither my mind nor self-esteem froze. Nor did I run. The new response happened so naturally and spontaneously that it wasn't until we'd worked through the episode satisfactorily and I was off the phone that I realized I had not frozen, fought, or flown. Whoopee. . . . Celebration time. And believe me, if I could learn to transform my fear by facing and embracing it, you can, too!

Freedom in Facing Feelings

The freedom that comes from being able to face our feelings can be so delicious. But it takes a lot of work, because we're all so poisoned by the conditioning that feelings are bad, especially the challenging, fiery ones. No matter how much work we do on ourselves, our judgments about our feelings often jump up and bite us. And so we push them back down. But we should know by now that denying feelings doesn't work. They merely go underground—into our subconscious and our physical bodies—until eventually we have to pay attention because they bring us physical and emotional dis-ease.

The feeling most responsible for blocking our way to hope is fear. Fear is different from discernment. Discernment is tiny, manageable doses of fear based on realistic concerns, such as the knowledge that it's dangerous to run out into traffic without looking. Discernment keeps us safe, makes us vigilant parents, gives us the drive to be activists for worthy causes, and makes law-abiding citizens of us. Fear, on the other hand, is the unrealistic, incapacitating stuff that limits our freedom severely. For instance, fear of rejection or ridicule can stifle our desire to express very valid ideas in business meetings or keep us in abusive or disrespectful relationships.

I would go so far as to say that fear is our only real enemy and avoidance is its most destructive collaborator.

Fear is the mother ship of all feeling.

Unchallenged, fear robs us of the very essence of our being, obscures hope, diminishes self-confidence, and stifles creativity. But we have the power to release it by facing it head-on. I learned this simple technique for embracing fear from Michael Toms, co-creator of New Dimensions Radio. When faced with a decision, Michael asks himself, "Am I making this decision out of fear or am I making it out of love?" A question such as this encourages us not only to face our fears when they arise but to actively go looking for them and bring them into the light of consciousness to be observed and transformed.

Courageously facing our feelings—with help, if

needed—is the first and most important step on the road to freedom and hope. Being aware of feelings enables us to transform them and, as a result, change reactions and actions that are no longer appropriate or desired.

A PRACTICE FOR EMBRACING YOUR FEELINGS

Be very gentle with yourself as you try this exercise. When we're facing our most painful feelings and fears, we're often dealing with very old stuff.

1. *Open to your feelings.* Become aware of your feelings by simply allowing them to surface. As you gently breathe in and out, open to the feelings that come.

2. *Embrace them.* Now embrace your feelings with great tenderness, as an unconditionally loving mother would. Whatever they are, just embrace them.

3. *Accept what is.* Honor and accept the feelings you're having *now*. Be gentle with yourself. Invite transformation to be the result of acceptance.

Inner awareness is the beginning of outer change.

The Strength in Surrender

What we're really talking about here is surrender. Not a depressed or hopeless "Oh, who cares?" sense of resignation, but a conscious choice to open to the unknown and step toward trusting ourselves and the Divine more deeply.

A client recently told me a story that struck my heart as a beautiful example of finding strength in surrender. A group of English women were incarcerated in a Japanese prison camp during World War II. Instead of succumbing to their despair, they decided to organize an a cappella choir that became so good they toured Europe when they were released. Instead of losing hope in the face of a gargantuan lemon, these courageous and inventive women chose to thrive and made some very potent lemonade in the process.

Another important kind of constructive surrender has to do with letting go of unrealistic and unrealized hope. If your hope of a different reality keeps bashing against a stone wall, it's probably time to give it up. Ivy, a dear friend of mine, was involved in a dreadful court case that essentially destroyed life as she and her family had known it, even after they were totally exonerated. After much agony, therapy, time, and soul searching she shared this thought: "I've finally come to realize that our hope cannot control, sway, or change others, and I have truly let go of what happened and am moving fully into life as it is now."

My friend's process of moving through a horribly unfair experience into the light of hope was not an easy or quick process and included periods of dark and debilitating depression plus a healthy dose of anger. However, by facing each feeling as she could, surrendering to her own vulnerability, and expressing, but not acting on, wishes for revenge, she now radiates strength, enthusiasm, and creativity. "It was hideous, horrible, and absolutely life changing. I wouldn't choose to go through what we did, but I sure like the qualities I've gained as a result of the experience," she says. As Ivy found out in a very hard way, we need to give up hopes rooted in the desire for other people to change.

Surrender is a difficult concept for a lot of us to grasp because our culture places such a premium on control and conquest. Surrender implies loss of control and being overpowered. And it is often exactly this fear of losing control that makes us deny our feelings and stuff our grief rather than working through issues as they arise. It's natural to fear that intense feelings will overwhelm you if you open yourself up, and that may actually happen for a while. In the long run, however, avoiding a feeling weakens us and renders the feeling much more powerful than surrendering to it does.

Because it takes tremendous energy to keep feelings at bay, the effort of resistance and avoidance is extremely stressful to both body and psyche. That's why it's so important to have support. If you want to work through scary feelings, don't try to go it alone. Talk with friends or professionals, take care of your body, and try to rest as much as possible.

Gifts in Tattered Wrappings

We can learn so much from pain. As therapist and author Merle Shain writes, "One often learns more from ten days of agony than from ten years of contentment." But we have to choose to have the learning experience and not be seduced into assuming the role of victim. We have to be vigilant. When we hear the victim rearing her head, muttering such questions as, "Why me?" it's up to us to retrieve the hopeful, optimistic aspect of ourselves. A victim cannot find the gifts inherent within pain because he or she is simply too invested in suffering and blaming to look.

Many gifts can eventually be found
among the tattered wrappings of distress.

I have a friend who has a great victim-busting approach.

When she feels her victim mind coming on, she allows 20 minutes to "mope, whine, blame, and feel sorry" for herself. Then she says, "Okay, dearie, let's see what we can learn from this!" It's pretty impressive that she gives this just 20 minutes, because we all know how easy it is to indulge in lamenting life's unfairness to poor little ol' me. Of course, what's important is the intention, not the time limit. If 20 minutes doesn't work for you, don't give up. It's still worth doing.

As a therapist, I have seen over and over again how difficult times provide people with the opportunity for growth spurts; that's why I now see them as incredible gifts. In my practice, I've heard so many people quote Charles Dickens's first line in *A Tale of Two Cities*—"It was the best of times; it was the worst of times"—when referring to some crisis they had weathered. Notice I said "weathered." It's almost always easier to see the best of times *after* the worst of the pain has passed.

As most of us have, I have experienced the growth-through-pain cycle countless times. After many years, I still marvel at and give thanks for the changes that occurred in me, and in my life, as a result of being divorced. Did it hurt? You bet! Did I hate it at the time and rile against it? Absolutely. Do I like the me I've become as a result of it better than the me I was before? Without a doubt.

Pain is often the incubator of compassion.

Isabel Allende writes, "The idea that we should avoid pain no matter what is crazy, because it separates us from the experience of the sacred. We are often in touch with the deepest part of ourselves through pain." That's it exactly. Being dragged through the knothole of grief and loss often draws people into the depths of their hearts where they discover a wellspring of unconditional love. John Tarrant, author of *The Light Inside Darkness*, says, "If I defer the grief I will diminish the gift." Like rough stones polished in a tumbler of pain, many of us emerge from intensely dark experiences more beautiful than before, endowed with greater understanding of ourselves and others and capable of deep and enduring love.

Pain can be a blessing in disguise—sometimes
in deep disguise—because it provides a portal
to spiritual and emotional insight and inspiration.

In his classic book *The Prophet*, Kahlil Gibran says, "Your pain is the breaking of the shell that encloses your understanding. Even as the stone of the fruit must break, that its heart may stand in the sun, so must you know pain." Whenever I'm working through my own pain, this passage gives me hope that some good will come of it. The wisdom of his words assures me that pain can offer many blessings among the bruises. Increased self-love and understanding, deeper and more meaningful relationships, and greater appreciation for all the wonders of life are a few blessings that spring to mind. Probably the most wonderful gift I've found among the tattered wrappings of pain is the gift of a heart more fully open to the warmth of the Beloved, as I often like to call God.

Repairing and Preparing the Ground of Our Being

It isn't for the moment you are struck that
you need courage, but for the long uphill
climb back to sanity and faith and security.
—ANNE MORROW LINDBERGH

How many of us are caught up in the whirlwind of life and don't even realize how bone tired we are? We push and push and push ourselves ever harder to perform, excel, overcome, be strong. I am reminded of the time I bought a new heart-shaped cookie cutter. After taking the price tag off, I scrubbed so hard at the gummy residue that I bent the heart. Hmmm. Don't we often scrub so vigorously at our perceived imperfections, weaknesses, and failures that we push our own fragile and tender hearts out of shape? What if we took a lesson from farmers' fields and gave ourselves permission to lie fallow for a while when we were spent and needed to replenish our store of emotional, physical, and spiritual energy?

When we notice we're running on empty,
it's time to refuel. Hope doesn't run on empty.

Many wounds happen quickly—someone we love dies suddenly, we lose our job without warning, the stock market greedily gobbles up our savings, or we receive a life-threatening diagnosis—while others like overwork, stress, and disaster-news-deluge happen gradually. Whether the tearing of the fabric of life as we know it, or wish it were, is quick or measured, repairing our spirits always takes time, effort, and concentration.

Individually, and as a society, we aren't good at allowing the time and space for repairing the ground of our being, and *preparing* it, for a new way of living after loss and pain. James Hollis, author of *Swamplands of the Soul* (I love that title!), says, "I am not what happened to me. I am what I chose to become." Ah, yes. I would add that the wisest decisions come only after allowing ourselves time to heal and replenish.

In order to receive and nurture any seeds of hope we sow, our hearts must be repaired and prepared.

Remembering and Befriending Self

To a great degree, hopelessness is a feeling of separation: separation from ourselves, others, our community, and our God. Far and away the most important connection each of us has is with our true Selves, but sometimes we've drifted so far from our authentic natures that we need to pause and intentionally remember who we really are: beautiful, incredible spiritual beings having a human, sometimes very difficult, experience.

A question used by cancer specialist Bernie Siegel can be a good check on how we feel about ourselves. He asks, "If God came in and said, 'I want you to be happy for the rest of your life,' what would you do?" Those of us who would honestly answer, "Bring it on, I can handle it *and* I deserve it!" are probably already great friends to ourselves. Most of us, however, would find ourselves hesitating or feeling undeserving or disbelieving. We could stand to do a bit of work on our friendship with the one closest to us.

I know I can have a hard time believing in my own goodness, so I surround myself with little heart-lifters to nudge my memory. For example, on my desk is a card that reads simply: *Remembering Who I Am*. To it, I've attached two other affirming statements. One from Chinese sage Lao-tzu states, "When you are content to be simply yourself and don't compare or compete, everybody will respect you." The other came from the wrapping on a piece of chocolate candy that appeared for the first time when I was feeling especially worthless and hopeless about a family situation. It says, "You are the star for which all evenings wait."

If you are able to remember your essence more easily than I, a straightforward comment such as "Whoops, I've forgotten who I am" may set you right back on track.

By consciously reconnecting with our true Selves, we can weed out feelings of hopelessness and cultivate feelings of hope.

Long ago I created the slogan, *Live gently with yourself and others*, for my business card because I badly needed to incorporate gentleness into my own life. It was easy for me to be gentle and accepting of my clients and family, but I often gave myself the short end of the kindness stick. Over the years, gentleness and acceptance have taken root in my heart, and I can truthfully say I'm a good friend to myself most of the time. Of course, I've had lots of help. If I revert to old habits now, my husband, Gene, will say, "Is that a gentle way to treat yourself?" Friends and kids do the same thing. In fact, friends and kids can be wonderful accomplices in helping us remember who we are. They can mirror our true Selves to us when our inner pools are too muddy to provide a true reflection.

A PRACTICE FOR BEFRIENDING YOURSELF

Take a few minutes to ponder the following questions:

1. In what ways could I be a better friend to myself?

2. How do I need to be more gentle and kind to myself?

3. Could I accept it if God said He/She wanted me to be happy for the rest of my life?

Allowing Friends and Family In

Because I was emotionally needy a lot of my life, I often asked for help but secretly felt ashamed of doing so and "bothering" my family and friends. I've come to believe, however, that being unwilling to receive is as stingy and withholding as is failing to give when appropriate and needed. As we so readily see during catastrophes, people want to be helpful. Giving makes us feel useful, therefore give-and-take is a good thing. Because receiving help facilitates and speeds up our healing process, we are able to share the fruits of love with others sooner.

Mother Teresa assured us, "Love is a fruit in season at all times." In fact, we all have so much sweetness we yearn to give each other. When we are able to receive help and support from family and friends, we give them a chance to share their fruits of love with us and give ourselves the opportunity to be nourished into healing. Refusing help from others, on the other hand, is a bit like saying, "I can't accept your fruit because it is sweeter than I deserve," or perhaps, "Your fruit isn't sweet enough for me."

Both the giving and receiving
of love and sweet support are gifts.

At church recently, the Old Testament scripture being read was the story of God giving Moses the power to strike a rock and provide water for the thirsty and grumbling Hebrews he was guiding to the Promised Land. Hearing that, I began to list people who have the power to metaphorically strike my rocks of sorrow and cause water to pour into my spirit when I'm crawling across a wasteland. God is the obvious answer, but so often She/He works through people. By the time church ended, I was saturated in gratitude for the wealth of friendship and water-providers I enjoy.

A PRACTICE IN REMEMBERING
WHO BRINGS YOU SOLACE AND SUPPORT

Please, take a little time to consider who strikes the rock for you when you are parched and in need of buoying by the waters of compassion, assistance, and acceptance. Who holds you in their heart when you are unable to hold yourself gently and tenderly? Who gives you the courage and will to keep on keeping on? Who leads you back to the well of inherent hope within you? I like to make two lists: one naming those who bring solace and support, and one that lists people to whom I provide the water of love and hope.

"Sometimes we have to break down in order to break through," a minister friend of mine said. This is true, but it is much safer and more productive to break down when help is standing nearby, ready to shore us up. Allowing friends and family into our hearts and souls during times of brokenness gives them the gift of being useful and gives us the gift of connection and support as we break through to the next step.

A PRACTICE FOR LIVING
MORE GENTLY WITH YOURSELF AND OTHERS

Jot down one or two tiny steps you could take today to begin to live more gently with yourself and, consequently, others. For instance, you might decide to stop being critical of yourself, or stop pushing yourself to do more than you're comfortable with, or speak up to someone who is treating you unfairly. Only you know how you can best befriend yourself and, in doing so, repair and replenish the ground of your being.

Of course, if your life is seriously out of control or you are acting in destructive or unkind ways, you may need help getting back in touch with your real Self. If you feel that out of touch, run—don't walk—to a therapist or group that can help you heal beliefs, wounds, or misunderstandings that are causing destructive behavior or despondency.

Resting and Reaping

There is a wonderful story about a few indigenous men who were acting as bearers for a group of European explorers. A few days into the trip, the bearers would not budge from the shade despite repeated protests and threats from their employers. Finally, they were able to make the explorers understand that in their culture they rested one day a week, without fail, in order "to let their souls catch up with their bodies." We, too, need to rest in order to reap the wisdom gathered through experiences, especially difficult experiences.

Immediately rushing on to the next thing, as we are prone to do, aborts the assimilation process by which we gain insight and growth from our pain. Instead, after an arduous climb through fear or pain, we need to stop and let our souls catch up with our bodies and invite understanding to catch up with our experience.

Resting on a learning plateau allows us to reap understanding from experience. It gives us time for "In Reach," "Up Reach," and "Out Reach," as my mentor, Annabelle, describes the spaces between experience, assimilation, and understanding.

In Reach: Inner exploration to sift and sort the lessons experiences offer and to reap understanding from them

Up Reach: Asking God to help us glean wisdom from experience and have the courage to make desired or needed changes

Out Reach: Empathetically reaching out to others going through similar struggles

Loving ourselves enough is the key to most everything.

For many years, my friend Bonnie and I led seminars for women. Because it's so easy, especially for women, to forget our own wisdom, we gave the women in our seminars cards that said, simply, *I know!* We do know. However, in order to know that we know, we need to take time to rest and listen deeply. By doing so, the wisdom of our hearts can catch up with, instruct, and replenish our bodies and emotions. That's how self-love is restored—from soft, silent attentiveness to inner whispers.

When we love ourselves enough, repairing and replenishing the ground of our being will be acceptable, listening to the wisdom of our hearts will become second nature—it was probably *first* nature before being leached away via pain, fear, and erroneous teachings—and trusting that we know what is good, right, and hopeful for us will be a given.

Living Lightly

A few years ago, out of a desire for more peace of mind and the need to address some health issues, my husband and I made a conscious decision to simplify our lives and lighten our attitudes. We adopted the "Less Is More" philosophy, with my own little twist: "Less is more . . . relaxing."

If we really want to, most of us can simplify and unclutter no matter what our ages or stages in life. With enough self-love and caring, we could choose to spend more time in overstuffed chairs and less juggling overstuffed schedules.

Just as too much demand placed on available electricity sources can result in citywide electrical brownouts, we, too, are light beings often overextended by demands of brighter, more long-lasting "shining" than we can manage. When depression and feelings of hopelessness set in, these are sure signs that our own circuits are overloaded: We experience physical, emotional, and spiritual brownouts.

"Turn your face to the sun and the shadows will fall behind you," a Maori proverb urges. What if you did turn your face to the sun and invited increased light and levity in your life? How might you feel if you lightened your load of commitments and accumulations, highlighted your attitudes and observations with humor, lowered your stress levels, and decreased demands for perfection and perform ance? More hopeful, perhaps?

If you were to turn your face to the sun and live more gently with yourself, what might you add or subtract from your life?

Patti, a minister friend, gave me a beautiful suggestion that has really helped lighten my life. She said, "I've decided that I'm tired of living under the yoke of perfectionism. My new motto is, *It's good enough!*" When I asked, naively, "What is?" she exclaimed, with the greatest enthusiasm, "Anything!"

Although I initially had my doubts about being able to incorporate an attitude of "good enough," it's actually been relatively easy and incredibly freeing. I encourage you to try it. If you're a visual person, you might try posting some "It's good enough" reminders around your house or office. I know this works for me.

In talking with Harriett, my table mate at watercolor class, I was struck by the impact hope and humor have in her life. "My husband has lived with cancer for the last eleven years, and hope is what keeps him positive," she shared. "Hope and a sense of humor have gotten him—us—through all the ordeals. We're out of treatment options now, so it's all hope and humor from now on." She then painted a beautiful sunset scene, because each sunset causes her "to be thankful for another day with the one I love." Harriett and her husband certainly know how to bring light into what, for many, could be a very dark situation.

Humor truly is one of the best sunbeams around. Humor lightens our hearts and increases the production of endorphins in our brains and bodies. Humor is the positive side of the "Ain't it awful!" coin. It heightens our awareness of the grace and goodness around us and helps us cope with ill will and malevolence. As author Anne Lamott says, "Laughter is carbonated holiness."

Giving Health a Boost

After a costly break-in at her home, a naturally upbeat woman responded to queries of how she was feeling by saying, "Pollyanna didn't have a stomach!" What a great answer. Though touched with humor, her honest response let people know that she and her stomach were very upset by all the destruction, loss, and upheaval in her home. Even when we wish we could deny that we're in physical and emotional pain, our bodies know better. Even when our mouths say, "Oh, I'm fine," our bodies respond honestly through discomfort, illness, and exhaustion. They are designed to process and express darkness and dis-ease. We would be wise to listen as they try to get our attention.

Well into the writing of this book, when I thought I'd overcome my initial fears about taking on a subject this big, I thought I might have a mild case of recurring flu because my tummy was queasy much of the time. In reality, I had denial-flu. After a two-year sabbatical, I was afraid I could no longer write, but I wasn't allowing myself to see the fear teasing my stomach. Neither my dreams nor my body believed the denial, however, and both continued to be uncomfortable until I faced my fear, embraced it, and began taking care of myself. As I honored my feelings, shared them with people I trusted, and moved through them as gently as I could, the light of hope began to peek through the clouds of doubt. Miraculously, I also recovered from the "flu."

As we learn to accept, honor, and constructively express our real feelings, our bodies will be free to maintain or return to health more efficiently and quickly.

My acupuncturist, Mary Ellen, taught me that Chinese medicine does not make distinctions between body, mind, and spirit but does teach that we all have different strengths and inclinations when our bodies experience a lack of health. There are people whose spirits never flag even during chronic or acute illness and others whose spirits crash at the slightest hint of illness. Mary Ellen and one of her sons fall into the latter group. She said, "We simply have to stop and go to bed even with a tiny sore throat. Although it can be annoying, it's the only way for us to return to health quickly." No matter which category you fall into, it's simply a matter of how you're made and not a cause for shame or pushing yourself beyond your ability to cope. Give yourself the gift of knowing and accepting how you're wired and your body the gift of a healing boost by acting accordingly.

Even though we all know that exercise is good for both body and soul, I want to touch on it briefly. Decorative snow globes provide a wonderful metaphor for the way exercise enlivens our bodies and lifts our spirits. They have to be moved in order for the glitter within them to show itself and sparkle. The same is true of our bodies. Without being moved and shaken a bit, the energy in our bodies and spirits settles to lower and lower levels. Stagnant energy causes a multitude of maladies, among them sleep difficulties, unrelenting stress, anxiety, hopelessness, perimenopausal symptoms, irritability, lethargy, loss of enthusiasm, and reduced sexual desire. When we become "movers and shakers" of our bodies, our health receives a much-needed boost.

In order to repair and replenish the ground of our being, and to express the hopeful sparkle inherent within, we need to energize the whole of our Selves— body, mind, emotions, and spirit.

Relaxing into Receiving and Recovering

We must lose our fear of rest. There are some of us
who keep our morale (morale being defined as
a belief in one's own cause) by being always busy.
We have made a fetish of fevered action.
—HOWARD THURMAN

Along with the adage, "It is more blessed to give than
to receive," many of us seem to believe another,
"Relaxing is the root of all evil." We feel so lazy or
indulgent at the very thought of putting our feet up to
rest. We recognize how good it is to give, but we're
lousy at receiving. But sometimes we have to allow ourselves to rest and relax into receiving and recovering to
give our bodies, minds, and emotions a space in which
to repair, replenish, and nourish seeds of hope. In order
to remind her "giver" self to receive, my friend Sue
moved her watch to her right wrist. She says, "It's so
uncomfortable but it keeps reminding me to shut my
mouth and open my left hand [the receiving hand in
many traditions] and graciously allow people to give to
me." Because Sue's husband is "fading away before [her]
eyes" it's especially important that she allow herself to
be loved, supported, and helped.

Let's add some new, loving and supportive beliefs to our repertoire:
It is as blessed to receive as to give *and*
Relaxation is the root of replenishing.

True relaxation and gracious receiving can give our lives and hearts a lift that is hard to imagine when we're fettered to a chain of overactivity, under-awareness, spiritual aridity, and a pull-yourself-up-by-your-own-bootstraps mentality.

Comforting Ourselves

Another way of becoming receptive is by learning to comfort ourselves. Other than chocolate, we may not know what comforts us or who within us needs comforting, but we can find out by gently looking within and asking ourselves what might feel comforting right now.

You may have noticed that I wrote *"who* within us." That's because several individual aspects of our whole Self are active within us at all times. Although they are called different things, I call them *sub-personalities.* When we are sad, angry, anxious, or scared, asking "Who in me is feeling this way?" is a straightforward way to get in touch with sub-personalities. Because I am a visual person, I usually "see" the part of me that needs my love. Very often it is either a child or a twentysomething young woman. One of my clients is more auditory, and she "hears" answers. Other people neither see nor hear messages but simply have a knowing about who within them needs comforting. It doesn't matter how we perceive our sub-personalities, only that we ask them what they want and need from us now, and then do our best to fulfill their requests.

Here's a very small example. The other day I was feeling stretched thin, both emotionally and time-wise, and ill equipped to handle all that needed to be accomplished. Even choosing what to wear seemed arduous. So, standing in my closet, I asked who was feeling so overwhelmed and "saw" a younger aspect of myself. She said she wanted and needed her mother. Since my mother died fifteen years ago, I asked my needy self if it would be enough to wear Mother's sweater and concentrate on feeling her love around us during the day. It was, and we did. All day I encouraged myself to feel wrapped in my mother's love and belief in me. Sustained by this love, I felt less alone and was able to concentrate on taking one tiny step at a time until most things were taken care of.

Jan, a wonderful client of mine who is in a very difficult marital situation, uses an image from one of her dreams to comfort herself when she doubts her ability to make the right decisions for herself and her daughter. In this dream, a queen was sitting on top of a hill receiving friends who had come to her for wisdom and counsel. Realizing that characters in dreams usually represent aspects of ourselves, Jan excitedly said, "Then all of the scared me's can come to the wise queen within me to find answers, can't they?" Yes, they can. We all have within us the wisdom and the compassion to comfort ourselves and prepare the ground of our being for sowing seeds of hope.

Another way we can comfort and rebuild ourselves is by affirming what we are aiming for. If I need reassurance of my goodness or worth, I use affirmations such as "I am a worthwhile and loving person even though I make mistakes. I create peace and harmony on our planet by first creating peace and harmony within myself." Or "I allow myself to rest in the unseen arms of God." At first our conscious mind will probably scoff at what it considers such blarney, but little by little our subconscious mind integrates the positive message, and we begin to feel more centered and peaceful.

Perhaps you are lucky in this regard, but patience is not my long suit. Therefore, in order to sidetrack the effects of impatience and obsession, I need little colleagues-in-consciousness reminders. One of my favorites is an Eastern aphorism Abe Lincoln quoted to the people of Illinois as he boarded the train for

Washington, D.C., to become president of a nation torn in two. It was, "And this, too, shall pass away." I have lain awake many nights assuring a quaking sub-personality that "This, too, shall pass" and "God is loving me now."

If none of the suggestions I've offered feels comforting to you, perhaps others sprinkled throughout these pages will resonate with your heart. If not, that's perfectly okay, too, because within you is a wise and compassionate sub-personality who does know how to soothe your spirit and quiet your mind.

A PRACTICE FOR DISCOVERING YOUR INTERNAL ALLIES

Take a moment and ask yourself, Who within me knows how to soothe my spirit and quiet my mind? What can she or he do to bring me comfort? Make a commitment to honor and act on the wisdom received.

Kicking It Upstairs

One of our best allies in sowing hope is God. By turning our concerns and ourselves over to God, we get a kind of shortcut to hope and healing. The expression "Let go and let God" reflects this idea. My friend and spiritual mother Annabelle calls it *Kicking it upstairs*. The idea of kicking something upstairs appeals to me because it is lightly touched with humor, and, since I'm not yet an A student in the letting-go department, I can always run up the stairs and fetch back my concerns if need be.

Of course, for many of us letting go is easier said than done. Even when we believe absolutely in the wisdom and healing inherent in letting go, our expectations of ourselves and others often make it difficult. Expectations come equipped with holding-on talons bearing stenciled admonishments such as, "I *should* be able to handle this!" or even worse, "I (they) *should* never have been/done/said blah, blah, blah in the first place!" The fear of letting go is resistance, plain and simple. Resistance to who we are, what is, and what might be.

Resistance—whether masked as anger, depression, or judgment—encloses our hearts in a steely vise and imprisons our souls in congealed fear. What a toxic environment for growing hope. That's why we need to "let go and let God" through prayer, affirmation, or empathy. Author Gail Sheehy writes, "Realizing that our safety does not reside in anyone else emboldens us to find security within ourselves." And, I would urge, also from a reliable spiritual source.

While I may not yet "kick" things upstairs easily and gracefully, I have found ways that help me drag my woes, and the woes of the world, up to God. Primarily, it's incredibly valuable to simply *remember* that you want to let go and let God handle what is impossible for you to sort and solve. For me, the first step in letting go is always expressing the feelings that rage or weep inside my soul by writing, painting, meditating, or just plain ranting. (My car is my rantmobile.) Second, I talk with trusted friends and family. I find that after the initial verbal release, inner work begins in earnest. Another way I ask for help kicking stuff upstairs is by singing prayers as I walk outdoors. I've learned to chant the Lord's Prayer in Jesus' native language, Aramaic. I like to dedicate the prayer to a certain concern or person and then chant it repeatedly; this brings great relief to my aching heart. I also make up songs depending on the issues I'm struggling with. Right now, my favorite letting-go song is "Thy will, not mine, Lord! Thy will not mine."

Most feelings that need to be released reside in the gut. Lifting "upset" energy from the solar plexus to the heart center is an extremely powerful letting-go and transformational tool.

Close your eyes and allow yourself to feel the energy boiling in your solar plexus area. See it as a symbol if that feels helpful to you. Ask angelic helpers, or any others that resonate with you, to help you lift the energy to your heart, where it can be transformed and sent out into the world as love or understanding.

Don't be surprised or disappointed if you can't do this right at first. Emotions are tenacious and don't like to budge easily. I've been doing this exercise for many years and still need to do it repeatedly with some feelings and situations before experiencing any movement at all. Perseverance usually pays off in the long run, and feelings do lighten and transform.

If this method doesn't work for you, I encourage you to find your own ways of kicking your concerns upstairs to the Beloved who loves you and longs to comfort and care for you.

Savoring Sleep

One of hope's most dependable colleagues is sleep. Sleep is the bringer of dreams, the mender of bodies, and the soother of spirits. Without the balm of gentle sleep, even tiny crises seem monumental and almost impossible to handle. Why, then, is it next to impossible to succumb to sleep when we are upset and need it most? Some people are simply non-sleepers, but most insomnia probably has a lot to do with the Rabid Thought Monkeys continuously yelling and leaping around on the branches of our brains. I bet you know the ones—those seemingly caffeinated voices that worry and blame and plan and scheme. The ones who tell you how horrible things are now and how much more horrible they are likely to become. The ones who berate and shame you. Some of us hear Worry Monkeys, others Regret Monkeys, Fear Monkeys, or the occasional friendly Excitement Monkey. It doesn't matter; all of them reject sleep.

Fortunately there are some wonderful, natural tranquilizers that can quiet the mind-monkey and allow us to savor the comfort and consolation of sleep. If upset or obsession is keeping you awake, you might try the following three-step routine:

A PRACTICE FOR INDUCING SLEEP

1. Siphon off the most persistent thoughts by writing them down and either tucking them away or tearing them up.

2. Do a few minutes of gentle stretches or light yoga exercises.

3. Drink a cup of warm milk with a dash of cinnamon.

Boulder, Colorado, psychotherapist and sleep expert, Dr. Richard Shane, teaches clients that a key to sleep is feeling safe, and that we can help ourselves feel safe by bringing our minds inside our bodies. Here are a few of his suggestions:

1. Allow your tongue to relax.

2. Gently feel the rise and fall of your chest without trying to change your breath.

3. As your chest becomes more comfortable, your mind can rest in that feeling.

According to Dr. Shane, this creates a feeling of safety, calming the body and mind into comfort/sleep mode, which signals the brain to shift into real sleep.

If sleep doesn't come after you've done everything you know to do, it's best to surrender to prayer and use the time to bless the planet and all others on your mind and heart. It's also a great time for gratitude. A friend of mine who often finds herself "bright-eyed and bushy-tailed" in the middle of the night says, "If I'm awake when everyone else seems to be asleep, I figure God needs me to pray, so that's what I do."

Sleep is an interior physician who gently heals our bodies, minds, emotions, and spirits. Invite her into your heart and bed and savor the comfort and healing she bestows.

Now that we've sown seeds of hope, it's time to watch as they tentatively send out tender young shoots to taste the sun and eventually bloom anew.

CHAPTER 3

Cultivating Hope

Beyond the barricades
               of mind and feeling,
Hope waits,
        in the heart,
Yearning to be
           welcomed home.
—AUTHOR

The other day I spotted a tiny pansy pushing its perky face out of a miniscule crack in a roadside curb. My walking buddy, Judith, and I stopped to congratulate "Pansy" on her ability to bloom in winter, especially in such an unlikely place. Pansy provided a curbside metaphor. Not only did her seed find enough sustenance among the concrete to survive, she also shared her beauty with two cold and weary women.

As Pansy did, we can create an environment within us that encourages seeds of hope to bloom and be shared. Pansy needed at least a few habitable features: a tiny amount of soil in which to set down tentative roots, a bit of sun, a minimal amount of water. Unlike Pansy's curb, our hope-growing habitat contains thoughts, feelings, and attitudes that are not cast in concrete and, therefore, can be cleared and transformed so they no longer obstruct our growth and happiness.

With awareness, intention, and effort,
we can cultivate a hope garden in our own hearts and minds.

I know it's possible to cultivate our inner gardens because my own mind used to be weed-ridden and uninviting to most anything except thorns and prickly pears. By taking time to access my true Self in the sanctuary of quiet and solitude, I have been able to dig up the weeds and grow more hopeful.

Weeding Our Minds

If you don't like what's happening in your life, change your mind.
—HIS HOLINESS THE DALAI LAMA

Where do all our internal weeds come from? As young children, without highly developed discernment skills, we absorbed erroneous messages such as "I'm not good enough, smart enough, good looking enough" from the world at large and the adults closest to us. Untrue and invalidating, these messages became our underlying assumptions and implicit beliefs and have continued to guide our lives. *Underlying* is the operative word, as these assumptions are *under* our conscious awareness and *lie* to us about reality. Since most of these values, beliefs, and attitudes are hidden, we are unaware of the extent to which they rule our actions and reactions.

Why do we believe these lies? Because our minds are two-faced. Both friend *and* foe. As friends, our minds are co-creators with God, taking us to great heights of creativity, love, and joy. As foes, they are destroyers of all we want and need and can cast us, quite literally, into a hell of hopelessness, self-destruction, and fear. The wonderful news is that we are not hapless victims of our minds' whims. In fact, our greatest God-given power is the power to *change* our minds. We can consciously search out the lies and transform them.

All products of the mind—thoughts, beliefs, assumptions, intentions, aspirations—are magnetic energy forms. Since like attracts like, darkness, despair, and fear attract actions, reactions, and circumstances with similar energy. For example, if we have the hidden belief that we don't measure up—it doesn't matter to what or to whom—we are likely to sabotage our ability to shine even in areas where we are multi- talented. If we believe that hideous adage, "Life is hard and then you die," sure enough. . . . Or, if we buy into the belief that the whole world is irretrievably going to hell in a handbasket, our little corner of it will probably be pretty hellish. Thankfully, the opposite is also true. Attitudes and beliefs that reflect light, love, and acceptance bring us more of the same. More often than not, this very simple principle takes oodles and scads of determination, desire, and stick-to-it-iveness to incorporate into our lives. But it is absolutely worth any effort it takes to turn our incredible minds into friends and playmates.

First, we must root out the limiting beliefs.

Uprooting Negatives: Planting Positives

One of the first things to know about uprooting negatives is that having negative thoughts is not shameful or an indication of poor character; it's simply a result of being human. We live, therefore we will, at least occasionally, have fearful and discouraging thoughts to deal with. Mark Twain helps us accept this truth by saying, "Courage is resistance to fear, mastery of fear—not absence of fear." I prefer the word *transformation* to *mastery*, but the idea is the same: Fear simply is. What we do with it is completely up to us.

I imagine there are some blessed people out there whose minds are like self-cleaning ovens and self-weed effortlessly, but most of us need to grub around in the unhealthy "fertilizer" of our thoughts in order to weed out the "Ain't it awful's," clear a patch of soil, and plant seeds of hope, love, and best-case scenarios. You might try the following weeding process:

A PRACTICE FOR WEEDING THE MIND

1. *Awareness.* Our thoughts create the feelings and emotions we experience in our bodies and souls. Bringing thoughts into the light of awareness gives us the opportunity to change them and, consequently, soften and sweeten the feelings they engender. All change begins with inner awareness.

a. When accosted by a difficult feeling, give your full attention to it. Gently explore the feeling rather than running from it or denying it. Ask yourself these questions:

   ▪ What am I feeling?

- Who inside me is carrying the feeling?
- What am I telling myself, in the privacy of my mind, that is feeding the feeling? (It helps to jot these down.)
- What fear is at the bottom of the feeling?

b. Accept yourself as you are right now—a person who is deciding what feelings and thoughts need pruning or pulling altogether. Give yourself credit for having the courage to make desired changes.

2. *Disidentification.* Although we have feelings, we are not our feelings. We are much more than the sum of our feelings and thoughts. Decide what and who you would like to be, and make up a sentence or two that describes the ideal—and real—you. Use the following sentence as a format:

I have this feeling of_____, but I am not this feeling. I am_____.

For instance, depending on the feeling, my affirmation might be, "I have this feeling of loneliness and separation, but I am not this feeling. I am a beloved child of God" or "I feel like a failure, but I am not this feeling. I am a worthwhile and loveable woman even though I make mistakes."

Disidentifying with our feelings allows us to step

out of the maelstrom of their intensity and develop an Observer's Eye. From this relatively objective place, we can choose to break the gerbil-on-its-wheel obsessive mindset and stop reacting from a wounded and worried part of ourselves. Our inner observer sees what needs to be healed as well as what is healing. By becoming a gentle and loving observer, we can stand apart from our feelings a smidge and affirm who we really are. Gently and supportively distancing from our feelings makes it much easier to change our minds and, as a result, make more constructive and self-loving choices.

3. *Affirmation.* Because our minds are highly sophisticated computers, they will continue to act in accordance with their programming until reprogrammed. Using affirmations is the easiest and most efficient means of reprogramming minds that I have found. When used consistently, affirmation transforms negation.

a. In order to convince our mind-computer that a new incoming command is genuine, affirmations are constructed as positive statements that are true now. Of course, affirmations are more quickly assimilated if your conscious mind can go, "Oh, goody! What a relief!" and then create a lovely mind picture that supports the affirmation, but most of us are prone to respond ironically, "Yeah, right!" when first using affirmations. Either way, given enough repetition, our subconscious minds finally accept the new "commands," and the affirmations take root and supplant the negatives.

At the onset, changing our minds is more a decision than a feeling. We decide to turn negative thoughts into positive, hopeful, and kindhearted ones because we know it serves our deepest desires, and our feelings—like puppies training to the leash—eventually get the hang of it and leap ahead, frolicking happily, or at least contentedly.

b. Examples of effective affirmations:

- I love myself. I am loveable.
- I have all the energy, talent, and enthusiasm it takes to make a good living.
- Peace lives in my heart of hearts.
- I am a loveable and worthwhile human being.
- I create peace and harmony on our planet by first creating peace and harmony within myself.
- I accept my mate (myself, him, her, it) as is.
- I am respectful of everything and everyone.
- Whether I can see it or not, the world is unfolding as it should.

- I am a good listener and a caring person.
- I make a difference.
- God is loving me now.
- I have all the time, energy, and skill to do what I want and need to do.

c. To create meaningful affirmations for yourself, review your answer to the question in the *Awareness* section, "What am I telling myself, in the privacy of my mind, that is feeding the feeling?" and then change those statements to constructive ones written as if they are true now. Let's say, for instance, you wrote, "The economy is going to get worse and worse. I won't be able to survive." How might you want to change that to a positive statement set in the here and now?

Play with this exercise. While it is a transformative change of mind and heart, it can also be fun. As you become aware of negative thoughts that are pulling you down, stop the cycle by congratulating yourself on noticing. "Good job, Self. Thank you for pointing this out." *Disidentify* with any feelings that are resulting from the thoughts:

"I have this feeling of_____, but I am not this feeling. I am_____."

And then consciously begin to repeat an *affirmation* that counteracts the negative thought you recognized.

As you become more adept at catching negative thoughts and transforming them through affirmation, you will be amazed at the uplifting difference it makes in your life, feelings, and attitudes. Like transforming "Ain't it awful!" to "Let's roll!" Awareness, disidentification, and affirmation are simple ideas that, like any good habit, take time to root and bear fruit. But when the affirmation habit does catch hold, how sweet it is.

Unplugging from Overload

Part of weeding our gardens means lightening our physical, mental, and emotional loads. In order to do that, we need to give up our robe and scepter and relinquish the crown of Master or Mistress of the Universe! I love the little letter making the e-mail rounds: "Today, you are not in charge of everyone and everything, everywhere. I am. Love, God." Although I chuckled when I first read it, I find myself using it a lot. It's an especially good one to remember when my jaws are clenched and I am efforting like mad to make something happen that I, as the Queen of the Universe, think appropriate. Simply telling myself that God is in charge, not me, is very comforting and helps me loosen my talons a bit and let go.

The fact is, much of our overload is self-chosen. We say "Yes" when our schedules and hearts cry out for "No." We take responsibility for other people's happiness, which is an exercise in futility, since we have very little control over anyone's happiness but our own. Hurrying keeps us stuck in one spot because we have no time for reflection. When facing challenges large and small we inundate our minds with "Ain't it awful" scenarios and thoughts instead of tuning to "What can I learn from this?" We allow our minds to become judgmental taskmasters and major critics rather than entertaining companions and perceptive counselors.

But, since we're in charge of plugging *into* overload, we are also totally capable of unplugging as well.

One of the most valuable "unpluggings" we can gift ourselves with is letting go of our own and others' unrealistic or unkind expectations. Doing a gentle "reality check" is very helpful in assessing expectations. For instance, I might say to my husband, "I need to do a reality check with you because I'm feeling like you're angry that I didn't get thus and so done today. Is that true?" If he isn't feeling angry or disappointed, I know I've assumed I knew what he was feeling and can let it go. If he is angry, he gets a chance to see if his expectations are a bit overbearing. Also, if you're looking at the to-do list you've given yourself for the day, you can ask yourself, "Is it realistic for me to expect to do all this stuff today—even if everything goes perfectly?" Sometimes simply questioning our expectations helps us see them as over-optimistic, to put it very gently.

The other day my house/life/self were all in an uproar. A handyman was noisily tearing the kitchen apart, a computer guru—speaking a new dialect of Cyber Garble—was attempting to train my non-cyber brain in an unlearnable program, clients were in crisis, and antifreeze was making a smelly blue puddle all over the garage floor. To augment the already stressful atmosphere, I added an internal litany against warmongering to the chaos. In the midst of all this, I qualified as a poster girl for the overloaded, weed-filled mind.

A bit of light broke through my dark thoughts as I was driving to get antifreeze. I remembered a simple breathing exercise: I could *choose* to breathe the concept of peace in, one breath at a time. Although shallow little strangles at first, my breath did begin to deepen and my overstretched nerves became a tad more relaxed. Back at home, I was able to semi-ignore the hammering handyman and approach my computer without shooting it six times and mounting it on the wall like a big game trophy, as a man in our town did this week.

If friends and family members are encouraging you to

attend weekly meetings of Angst Anonymous, it's a safe bet you are suffering from Information, Acquisition, Expectation, and Stimulation Overload. Please remember that you, and only you, can pull the plug.

> *We can choose to unplug from overload, one decision,*
> *one thought, one breath, one step at a time.*

Acting As If

Hope is a thirsty flower that thrives best when consistently watered by an optimistic mind. So what do we do when we're not feeling so very optimistic? We can always pretend. Sometimes acting *as if* something were true allows it to become a reality in the realm of feeling and emotion. The intention creates the reality. John Wesley, the minister who founded the United Methodist Church, encouraged himself and other ministers to "Preach until you believe." Rev. Wesley preached continually but, nonetheless, floundered in his faith until well into his ministry when he experienced a "warming of the heart." I can only guess that John Wesley hoped he would eventually find the faith he wanted and, as a result, preached and acted *as if* it were true until his hope became a reality.

Acting *as if* isn't cheating, it's simply making a decision to opt for "up" rather than "down."

For example, even when only mouth-deep, a smile can lift our spirits, especially when it's returned. Strangers are good people to practice on because they take us at face and smile value. Walking around a little lake recently, feeling as low as a turtle tummy, I decided to practice "as if" on the woman walking toward me. Generating a grin, I said, "Aren't we lucky to have a place like this to walk?!" Her return smile and comment were so upbeat that I felt my mood elevate in response. And I found myself seeing my surroundings with a heightened sense of appreciation and feeling luckier and more upbeat as a result.

Our minds are indiscriminate eaters.
What we feed them, they will believe.

This Christmas, Tamilou, a friend of ours, befriended Jamie, a homeless woman who regularly panhandled at a busy intersection. Jamie was hard to miss as she cheerfully waved at cars with her Santa hat bobbing in the breeze. The sign she held was positive, beautifully printed, and explained, "Single mother waiting for disability. Anything to tide us over is appreciated. Merry Christmas!" Even though she had recently been released from the hospital after months of rehab for burns over much of her body, lost her home and job as a result, slept in her car, and didn't fit Social Services' criteria for help, Jamie flatly refused her sixteen-year-old son's offer to quit school and support them. Instead, she stood in the cold, wind, and occasional snow absolutely looking and acting as if she were Mrs. Santa, whose job it was to cheer up drivers.

Jamie provides us with a wonderful reminder that no one can force-feed our minds. The thoughts, beliefs, and assumptions we feed them are entirely up to us. We can either "feed the hand that bites us" by allowing negatives to overgrow and overwhelm us, or we can uproot negatives, plant positives, unplug from overload, and practice acting as if when appropriate. By cultivating hope through cleaning up the gardens of our minds, we bring more beauty and light to ourselves, others, and to our beleaguered planet, all of which can certainly use as much hope and compassion as we can muster.

Enriching Attitude and Intention

Observe your thoughts; they become your words.
Observe your words; they become actions.
Observe your actions; they become habits.
Observe your habits; they become your character.
Observe your character; it becomes your destiny.
—FRANK OUTLAW

I'm sure we're all familiar with the popular aphorism, "Attitude is everything." I suggest that attitude is actually the *beginning* of everything and walks hand in hand with intention in the process of cultivating hope, increasing peace of mind, and bringing desired changes into being. Attitude and intention, in concert with thought and awareness, can either guide us on the paths our souls long to take or distract us from the meaning and joy we are here to find and share.

The richer, deeper, and more compassionate our attitudes and intentions, the easier it is to find hope in the midst of despair and share love in the midst of sorrow and fear.

Metaphorically speaking, we might think of attitude as the watertight rowboat in which we bob and intention the oars that propel us to a desired destination. Attitude keeps us afloat while intention gets us going. Both are equally important companions throughout life's journey.

Clarifying Intention

Intention is a commitment or agreement to put once-vague ideas or desires into practice. It is thought solidified. Clarifying our intentions gives us a guide upon which we can base decisions and set goals. For instance, if we hold in our hearts a clear intention to live honestly, each time an opportunity to be even a tiny bit dishonest presents itself, our intention makes our decision an easy one. Let's say, a clerk gives you change for a $20 bill when you gave her a ten. Returning the extra money is the obvious decision if you are to stay in integrity with your intention.

Maureen, a single mom, gives us a good example of goal and intentions working hand in hand. With the help of a vocational counselor, Maureen explored how much money she needed for her family and what career she might truly enjoy that would support them. Being a dental assistant fit the bill. With her intention to become a dental assistant firmly in mind, Maureen outlined realistic goals to bring her dream to fruition and made decisions that brought her closer to her goal. "I wrote down my intention, talked it over with my kids, and then together we outlined our goals on a poster board and hung it in the kitchen." With a laugh, Maureen said the kids were great at asking, "Is this decision going to get us closer to our goals?" What a smart woman and great mom to make her intention a family goal and project.

It is intention that makes dreams come true; intention that abolishes slavery and institutes civil rights; intention that makes relationships work—with ourselves as well as others. Intention creates works of art and scientific advancements, clears a path toward desired goals, and gives us the courage and energy to keep on keepin' on when the going gets tough.

Recently I realized I'd made myself unhappy by wallowing in "what if's" and "oh good grief's" over a family situation. My unhappiness had not improved the situation one iota. Gently taking myself by the scruff of the neck, I set my intention to be happy (or at least peaceful) no matter what was happening, or did happen, with the situation. Having set the intention, I next began to change my attitude from "Woe-is-we" to one of gratitude and affirmation for the growth I believe can come from such situations. Every time my Rat Terrier Mind began to gnaw on the same worries, I remembered my intention and changed the channel from Enemy Mind to Friend Mind and repeated the affirmations I'd created for this situation.

Remembering my intention got me out of the cul-de-sac of sadness and back on the track to happiness and peace of mind. Eventually, grace began to pierce the fog of fear and disappointment, and a few rays of light shone through. By the time the person whom I most needed to hear from did call, I was already feeling pretty happy. Her call made it better, of course, but my happiness did not hinge on it.

That intention was circumstance specific; often our intentions are more global in nature. For instance, when my client Deirdre was feeling hopeless and depressed and noticed that she'd drifted into a sense of separation from her Source, she set an intention to feel closer and more attuned to God. Each morning she prayed, "Please help me remember my intention to be closer to you today. Thank you." To help support her intention, she decided to take a walk during her lunch break instead of sitting with coworkers who often used their free time to air grievances about work. Because she found singing uplifting, she decided to sing a chant as she walked: "Lord, I am thine, I am thine. . . . Make me thine, make me thine. . . . I am thine, I am thine."

These words were directly aligned with her intention.

Then Deirdre added old hymns to her repertoire and made up her own heart-songs as she walked. Intuitively, Deirdre did the perfect things to support her intention. She started her day connecting with God and asking for help, absented herself from negativity, affirmed what she longed for via song (we absorb words well when they are set to music—think of the old commercial jingles you can easily remember), and she shared her lighter heart and feelings of deeper spiritual connection with people who cared for her.

A PRACTICE FOR SETTING AN INTENTION

Find the time to focus on what you really would like to have more—or less—of in your life. Only you really know what will bring a sense of joy, hope, and fulfillment into your heart. Perhaps you would like to feel more hopeful. Perhaps you would like to serve others more often. Perhaps you would like more education, a better relationship with your mate or children, to help the world in some way, or to be more openhearted. Make a list of your heart-held desires and ponder what intention you could set to begin bringing them to fruition. It often helps to set an umbrella intention and then to break any action into small steps. Sometimes itsy, teensy steps. For instance, if your intention is to get more education, clarify what type of education you would like, and today make one phone call or read one catalog that gives you a little more information.

Setting intentions is like laser surgery for the soul. When we:

- Decide what we want
- Focus attention on it
- Act in accordance with our intention
- Cultivate an attitude that supports the intention

the Universe often responds by saying, "Okay!"

Saint Francis is said to have originated the phrase, "Hell is full of good intentions or desires," which we now know as, "The road to hell is paved with good intentions." Yes, good intentions left to languish can lead to regret, which is, indeed, very hellish. Conversely, when we clarify our intentions and set them in motion, the results can be heavenly.

Gentling Attitude

Remember, attitude and intention are boat and oars. Without oars, the boat might not move, but with holes in our boat, we just sink. At this very moment our less-than-gentle attitudes about ourselves and the world are drilling holes in our boat.

Trouble is, most of us were not raised believing that being gentle with ourselves was optimal behavior, and we certainly are not living in a gentle world right now. Of course, there are wonderful attitudes and areas of gentleness everywhere. But, because of media blight and the very real plight of so many people, we often need to search for the grace of gentleness. It is out there, and, more important, we can create it *inside* our own selves. Even better, with gentleness as our internal guide, we can become emissaries of gentleness elsewhere.

The first step in gentling our attitudes is to be aware if they are a bit rough around the edges. With awareness, we can set our intention to act differently. We might say, "My intention is to be gentle and kind to myself at all times and in all situations." You can also create an affirmation such as "I am gentle and kind to myself" to support your intention.

Like flowers, we thrive, grow, and bloom into our highest potential more readily in a gentle and nourishing environment. Our inner environment is the most important greenhouse we have.

Another way to gentle attitudes is to have some ready-made affirmations to call on. Some good ones include:

- This, too, shall pass.
- I can do all things through God who strengthens me.
- "It is always darkest just before the day dawneth" by Thomas Fuller.
- Anything I go through, I can *grow* through.

And the powerful and empowering:

- Please help me. Please help them. Please help us. And thank you. Thank you. Thank you.

Believing in Benevolence

Everywhere we turn, we are inundated by newspaper stories, television reports, nasty "reality" programs, and radio talk show tirades that emphasize malevolence. However, none of these shows or programs would survive were it not for our own mind's fascination with the frightful. In order to cultivate hope, we need to turn away from this steady diet of disaster and doomsday depression and, instead, bolster a belief in an overarching benevolence at work in the universe. I'm not advocating ostrich-like ignorance, but I am saying that too much emphasis on the negative simply invites more negative into our hearts, minds, and world.

Another downside is that our children readily pick up on our attitudes and feelings. If we are anxious and hopeless, it can scare our children and rob them of some of the wonder and joy of childhood.

In essence, believing in benevolence is a return to trust. I'm talking about setting our intention and tuning our minds and hearts to trusting in God and in ourselves, not blindly trusting the outside world, which often simply sets us up for disappointment and disillusionment. Chinese philosopher Lao-tzu gives us a beautiful affirmation for trust: *Open yourself to heaven and earth, then trust your natural responses. Everything will fall in place.*

I know that trust is hard to come by when hope is hollow. As a result, we'll probably have to act *as if* we have hope and trust long before we actually feel it. Inevitably, consciously opening ourselves to God and making a commitment to connect with our higher Selves will put our feet back on the path to trust.

As I was walking a labyrinth with a small group of women recently, I passed Juliette, whom I knew had been having a difficult time. Because she was crying, I stopped walking and hugged her. She burst into sobs, but between them whispered, "I'm really okay." I believed her, because I know her well enough to know that her spiritual beliefs are embedded in a solid foundation of trust in God and a growing realization that she can also trust herself. Like Juliette, we can weave trust so snugly into the fabric of our being that we will be okay no matter how not-okay we might feel and appear today.

Enriching our trust does not mean that we will be spared the storms of life. Not at all. Even though our Attitude-of-Trust boat can seem very flimsy during the harshest storms, we nonetheless survive churning waves best when held in the safety of trust and life-jacketed by the intention to grow through all of life's turmoil.

My friend Mugs uses a little ritual to help her inflate her attitudes and intentions when they begin to lose their oomph and limp around like week-old helium balloons. "I say to myself, 'Okay, Self, go find something good to concentrate on!'" She then sets her intention to see signs of benevolence wherever she looks. "There's *always* something when I decide to look":

sunrises, her dog and cat, flowers, babies, sleep, kindness of friends and strangers, the moon, clerks who are friendly and helpful, memories, and gratitude. Since the recent drowning death of a dear friend, breath itself has become a sign of benevolence to Mugs.

If you have temporarily lost track of trust and a belief in benevolence, you might try the following prayer, which was written in 1941 by James Dillet Freeman. I first saw it in a church booklet and liked it so much that it became a part of bedtime prayers for all my children. The tradition continues as our daughter now says it with her sons.

> The light of God surrounds me;
> The love of God enfolds me;
> The power of God protects me;
> The presence of God watches over me.
> Wherever I am, God is!

A PRACTICE FOR RESTORING YOUR BELIEF IN BENEVOLENCE

Think of things that help restore your belief in benevolence. Does reading uplifting books and articles help you? Surrounding yourself with friends? Being in nature? Meditating? Going to movies? Creating something beautiful? Cooking? Whatever buoys your spirit, make a commitment to turn to it the next time you need a trust and benevolence booster.

Accessing Self through Quiet and Solitude

Solitude is the furnace of transformation. Without solitude we remain victims of society and continue to be entangled in the illusions of the false self.
—HENRI NOUWEN

Several years ago the staff of our counseling center went to the island of Hawaii for a workshop with Dr. Elisabeth Kübler-Ross, eminent teacher about death and dying. Surrounded by colleagues I loved and respected and stimulated by spiritual ideas and energy, I was able to remember, and feel, the oneness of God and Her children, myself included. I felt that, if even just for a moment, I was able to access my authentic Self.

Paradoxically, this incredible sense of knowingness was accompanied by a feeling of homesickness, and I craved silence and solitude in which to absorb and appreciate the wonder of connection with the Beloved.

While others slept, I sought out solitude under the silent stars. Alone in the quiet, I immersed myself in an indescribable sense of being at home in God. It was heaven. Or at least a preview of coming attractions, and it was only possible because I eliminated distractions.

The authentic Self is never without hope, because it is inseparable from God who is love. Centered in love, the light of hope is not obscured by a fog of fear. On the other hand, the false self is at the mercy of circumstances, events, and our own inner turmoil. The false self forgets its spiritual connection and believes the personality we wear for this particular earthly sojourn is all we are.

I wish I could say that the luscious feeling of connection I felt with my authentic Self in Hawaii still comes back at a moment's notice, but it doesn't. What I can do is access the memory of how whole, complete, and uncomplicated I felt at the time. More often than not, simply remembering feeling absorbed in and loved by God is enough to bring hope and hints of happiness into my heart.

Carl G. Jung came to understand the need for connection and communion with God more deeply as he aged. He wrote, "The longer I live the more I realize the central question has to do with God and my relationship to this super-reality." The sweetness of solitude and quiet can enrich our relationships with the super-reality upon whom our authentic Selves are modeled.

Like fish need water in which to swim and birds need sky in which to fly, we need the peace of stillness and solitude in order to thrive. In the arms of quiet and solitude, we can hear the sweet voice of soul.

Defragmenting Inner Hard Drives

Of course, if our minds are fastened on fear and running amok in a weed-ridden forest of negative thoughts, solitude and quiet can sometimes exacerbate feelings of anxiety, isolation, and depression. Attempting to find peace and hope in quiet and solitude when your mind is overloaded and in Enemy Thinking Zone is like trying to get your computer to run even though the hard drive is fragmented. A couple of days ago, after giving me some written messages that were equivalent to rude gestures, my computer refused to budge. I begged it, prayed over it, sent it energy, kicked it, and finally turned it off illegally. Zilch, zero, nada. . . . Then I remembered the message: "Your hard drive is fragmented."

I'm not a cyber whiz by any stretch of the imagination, so my son gave me a Simple Simon explanation of fragmented drives. He said that a whole lot of information has been stored hither and yon on the hard drive until it is so fragmented it can't make sense out of anything and simply stops. I would translate this as, The guts of the machine get so stressed out and discombobulated that it has a nervous breakdown. (As a writer, my own breakdown has been known to follow quickly thereafter!) In its wisdom, the computer knows that it needs to lower its stress level and organize all the bits and bytes into a form it can comprehend before it will have the resources to continue.

Ah ha! I got it. How about you? There is so much stored within our minds, emotions, psyches, and subconscious that many of us are fragmented beyond tolerance levels, and stress is a very real concern for us all.

If we feel fragmented, chances are little scraps of our energy—from today, plans for tomorrow, regrets from yesterday, fears of the future—have gotten hooked on difficulties and stored every which way in our minds and hearts, making it nearly impossible to access our true Selves. We, too, need to "defrag."

The *Wall Street Journal* recently featured an article entitled "Are You Stressed Out Yet?" In studying the problems of stress, the writer discovered,

> The new research—which has been fueled in part by national stresses of Sept. 11—is exploring how some people manage to glide through

stressful situations, while other wind themselves tighter as the day goes on.

It isn't that the first group is spending more time at the day spas. It isn't even that they are confronted by less stress. Researchers have pegged stress resistance to a single quality: resilience. People who handle stress well recover quickly, physically and mentally, when confronted by it. From the way they breathe at their desks to how much they laugh, they engage in a set of subtle behaviors that help them shift easily in and out of "stress mode" throughout the day.

Subtle behaviors such as

- Taking a few deep belly-breaths
- Changing negative mind chatter to positive self-talk
- Saying a quick prayer
- Closing our eyes for even a minute of quiet gratitude

all help us move out of stress mode. They quiet our minds and slow our heart rates. They help us break the domino effect an over-accumulation of stress can produce in our physical, emotional, mental, and spiritual bodies.

Beyond this simple list, what else can we do to defragment our inner hard drives? One fun friend of mine wrote the words *Duck Feathers* on a piece of paper to remind her to let more stuff roll off her back. You might have one that reminded you to *Breathe....Stretch.*

There are as many ways to be resilient as there are people. My niece centers herself and gets rid of troublesome energy by running, walking, or lifting weights. Among other things, I read mystery and *Star Trek: Next Generation* novels. Many people, women especially, talk with friends. An artist I know goes into her "paint zone." Another friend meditates and prays as she does needlepoint pieces. Of course, there are less constructive methods of defragmenting. Overindulging in food, drink, or television are some favorites. Some kids in our neighborhood have resorted to vandalism, which I believe might be their unconscious attempt at defragmenting.

Here are some other techniques:

NINE PRACTICES FOR DEFRAGMENTING YOUR INNER HARD DRIVE

1. Write down bothersome thoughts. Release them by burning, tearing, trashing, or putting in a little jar of water in the freezer (put 'em on ice!).

2. Take a shower and imagine chaos and concern washing out of and off your body and mind and flowing down the drain.

3. Become a loving parent to yourself by giving the needy aspects of your personality what she or he longs for.

4. Say, write, or sing affirmations.

5. Lie on the floor with your feet against the wall perpendicular to your body for a few minutes.

6. Breathe deeply and slowly into your heart and belly. Exhale worries and cares, and inhale support and love.

7. Read something soothing and uplifting.

8. Lead yourself in this prayerful intention created by my friend, Annabelle:

Gently close your eyes and allow an image or sense of your body, mind, and emotions to come into the theater of your mind. Are they bouncing around like Lotto balls, or are they calm, serene, and aligned with each other?

Imagine that a beautiful, calming light is resting over your head, bathing your body, mind, and emotions in its warm and soothing light. Now repeat the word *Together* three times in sets of three.

"Together, together, together ..."
"Together, together, together ..."
"Together, together, together ..."

Without judgment, watch your body, mind, and emotion images and—without forcing—encourage them to come into alignment, under the light. Repeat "Together, together, together ..." as often as necessary.

9. Choose one or two ways to help you be more resilient to stress and strain and set your intention to use them as needed.

Whatever you choose to do, remember that great joy and renewal can be found in the sweet sanctuary of quiet and solitude.

Renewing in the Stillness

I was tempted to leave this section blank. No words. Simply the restful stillness of white space. . . . However, I'm a writer and I feel compelled to fill the space with words.

All this talk of quiet and solitude is nice, but who among us gets to have *that* on any regular basis? Even those who live extremely privileged lives are by and large deprived of silence and solitude. Noise and incessant demands are our constant companions. How can our spiritual Selves make their still, small voices heard amid the din? How can the higher and deeper ideas, feelings, and intuitions emanating from our souls get through the static of hectic daily lives? They can't, unless we stop and incorporate the 3 Rs—rest, renewal, restoration—into our schedules.

We're all aware that rest is necessary for both body and soul and that being sleep-deprived is as close to bona fide craziness as we ever hope to come. Although we probably will not go insane, without quiet, reflective spaces in which to rest our souls, open to inspiration, and be refreshed and renewed, we can definitely become confused, bewildered, and hopeless. Being still allows the murky waters of our minds to clear and invites the light of heart and soul to shine on and from our inner and outer lives.

Resting in the Sanctuary of Solitude

In solitude,
Soul finds her voice
And sings
our unique songs.

In solitude,
Soul guides us toward
   Personal paths of
serenity, surrender, and service.

   In the sacred sweetness
of solitude,
   Soul unveils
our true selves.

One might think I was in a state of bliss as I wrote this poem, but that's not true. I was not only grieving deeply over the death of a dear friend, I was also having a profound crisis of confidence. Groping blindly in this dark pit, everything about me came under scrutiny. Work, family, ad infinitum. . . . Thankfully, I did have the luxury—no, the necessity —of solitude.

You see, solitude offers several forms of sanctuary. The solace of connecting with our authentic Self, which is, in essence, a simple self: a self who laughs easily and relishes time to bask in nature, enjoy the smile of a child, and rest in the embrace of the Beloved. Such solitude feels like being safely and snugly wrapped in a down quilt on a silent, snowy night. But I have also found that it is only when quiet and alone—free from the extraneous—that we are able to become aware of the toxic beliefs we hold and jettison behaviors that are no longer beneficial to us.

Rest assured, stillness and solitude are not usually treks into a burning desert but, instead, serve as respites from overload and as uninterrupted opportunities to access the beauty of our soul-selves. Contrary to what we may imagine, taking time for solitude is one of the best ways to restore a feeling of connection with others and with God. Anne Morrow Lindbergh says, "Only when one is connected to one's own core is one connected to others. . . . And, for me, the core, the inner spring, can best be refound through solitude."

Simply removing ourselves from the fray and being in our own energy for a while gives us the opportunity to open to and bask in a sense of oneness with our creator, ourselves, and others. Waiting within the sanctuary of solitude is the still, small voice of soul whose joy it is to lead you to the center of your being where love, hope, and serenity abide.

CHAPTER 4

HARVESTING HOPE

A little bit of
        heaven
Can be gleaned from
           every day.
—AUTHOR

There are days when hope seems hidden in a bramble bush, its fruits invisible to our harried hearts. At such times it's important that we turn our faces to the light, stay in the present moment, and look for outer and inner glimmers of grace and hope. Today, a friend and I found something hopeful growing in the crevasse of a beautiful Colorado boulder: a six-inch pine sapling. Obviously, the seed had fallen in a rocky, hard place, taken root in spite of its environment, and was sweetly (and, it seemed to me, a bit cockily) basking in the sun for us to enjoy and learn from. I hope I can remember this tiny tree the next time I feel stuck between a rock and a hard place and wonder how on earth I can bloom there.

Noticing that little tree growing in the boulder is one way of harvesting hope. Some days will yield only a tiny basket of positives, while others will present fields of daisies in which to dance. No matter what the yield, focusing on recognizing and cherishing each little hope as it is offered lightens our hearts.

Empowering the Present

I've always had two or more tracks running in my head. The pleasurable one was thinking forward to some future scene. Imagining what should be, planning on the edge of fantasy. The other played underneath with all too realistic fragments of what I should have done. There it was in perfect microcosm, the past and the future coming together to squeeze out the present— which is the only time in which we can be fully alive. . . .
—GLORIA STEINEM

Recently I was talking to a young friend who was terrified that her newly purchased business was going to fail and her future would be in ruins. Her concerns are well founded, and, after listening for a while, I asked, "Honey, can you manage only what needs to be done *right now?*" After some hesitation, she answered, "Yesss. . . ." My friend had fallen into what I call the Future Hole. Her fear of a *possible* future was paralyzing her ability to be positive *now*. The enormity of possible future losses was also causing her to panic. How well I recognize the Future Hole/ Panic scenario from my own life. Do you?

When we're feeling confused, chaotic, or discouraged, focusing on something that is orderly *right now* helps us regain equilibrium. By finding order in the present moment—and in close proximity—our minds can realign to accept the possibility of order being available elsewhere.

Closely examining the center of a flower and noticing the incredible order and beauty in it gives us hope. Even looking for the orderly progression of words on this page, or observing how predictably your fingers flow from the palms of your hands, can bring solace when you are assailed by chaos and hopelessness. Allow yourself to be calmed by the order and do-ability inherent in the present moment.

By consciously working with the feelings and patterns active in the *present*, we also heal wounds and misconceptions from the past. Freed from the limits of the past, we can choose new, self-loving, and affirming ways to live and love in the world. Now is truly the only moment in which we are fully alive. To paraphrase a popular aphorism, "The present moment: use it or lose it."

While we can heal the past and influence the future,
we are only fully alive and empowered in the present.

Right now, this minute, is all we are required to handle. More than likely we can make it through what needs doing, being, or feeling when we stay out of the impotency of the Future Hole or Past Regrets and concentrate on the moment at hand. On the bright side, when we tune our hearts and minds to our abundant blessings, the present minute also overflows with much to appreciate, enjoy, be grateful for, and find hope in. Right here, right now, all that is good, true, and beautiful, all that is hopeful lives in our hearts.

Simply remembering to empower the present helps us find soothing order and structure in our bodies and our environments each and every minute.

One word of caution: Because most of us are so accustomed to squandering the present by rummaging around in our past and projecting our thoughts into imagined future scenarios, it's essential that we be gentle with ourselves as we focus on the new habit of empowering the present. It won't help to chastise yourself for falling into a Future Hole or for traipsing into the Realm of Regret; it will simply make you more clever at hiding your future and past forays from yourself. Go gently.

Given time, effort, and intention, you will be able to live in the empowered moment, just as Gloria Steinem has learned to do: "These past and future tracks have gradually dimmed until they are rarely heard. More and more, there is only the full, glorious, alive-in-the-moment, don't-give-a-damn yet caring-for-every-thing sense of the right now."

Changing any pattern is more easily done in a climate of caring support than it is in the glare of criticism.

Pausing to Appreciate

Pausing is one gentle way to train ourselves to lean more and more into this day, this hour, this moment. Remembering the adage, "We don't remember days, we remember moments. Life is made up of moments," can help us pause and appreciate what's going on right now.

A PRACTICE IN APPRECIATION

Just for fun, take a moment right now to look around—or within—with appreciation. Right this minute, I am telling myself: I appreciate the rain soothing our drought-stricken state. I also appreciate being snug and warm inside my home. What about you? What little bit of heaven is presenting itself to you right now? How can appreciation help you empower and enjoy this tiny little oasis of time? What feeling of hopeful appreciation is ripe and ready for harvesting in this very moment?

I love the pithy statement, "Wherever you are, be there!" Not being where we are right now is being away from home. Home is the empowered present. Home is choosing to come from our hearts *now*. Victoria, a friend of mine who has been living with an incurable and unpredictable form of cancer for two years, says she's a much different person than she was before cancer became her companion. "How so?" I asked.

"Well, I'm a much softer person than I was. And I'm much more here than I used to be." She elaborated, "I was always somewhere else. . . . Oh, my body was there and I could fake being present really well but my mind was usually a thousand miles away and I really didn't see the people I was with. In fact, they sort of annoyed me. Now I truly see the person right in front of me. I'm much more attentive, much more present than I ever was before. Each minute, each person, each animal . . .

and me . . . we all seem so much more precious now."

Each moment is born anew when we pay attention to
and embrace it. Each moment missed is a moment gone.

Cancer drop-kicked Victoria into a desire to be present to each moment and the people in it. Actually, I've noticed that the ability to empower the present is shared by many people living with life-threatening or life-altering illnesses. In truth, life itself is a life-threatening state, and each of us has a finite number of moments to live on Earth. Even without a cosmic kick to the derriere, we can make a choice to notice momentary wonders that stoke the fires of hope in our hearts. We can truly *be with* ourselves and others, we can savor the clarity of a flash of inspiration or understanding, we can see coincidences as gifts from above.

In being where we are, we can turn one tiny moment
of appreciation or prayer into the serene eye of a storm
or a private sanctuary of encouragement and acceptance.

Literally thousands of times a day we have the power to choose pausing in the moment, noticing its truth, and accepting the gifts and lessons it offers. We have the option to be fully alive in the here and now.

Embracing Compassionate Detachment

Because it throws us into a past and future over which we have absolutely no control, one of the best ways to *disempower* the present is to be overly attached to other people's chaos and try to *fix* it for them. While caring for others is essential, it's equally important that we not carry their feelings as our own. I first learned the value of compassionate detachment as a neophyte therapist who, unschooled in the art of detachment, carried all my clients and their challenges home in an emotional backpack. After a few months, I was exhausted and overwhelmed by all the baggage I'd collected. I even wondered if I were ill suited to the counseling profession. Luckily, a seasoned therapist shared the concept of compassionate detachment with me and gave me some pointers on incorporating it into my practice.

Even canine parents have a hard time being lovingly detached. A few years ago, our dog, Johnny, did not return from a walk in the woods with Gene. We thought she'd been sidetracked chasing a squirrel and would return shortly. As the day wore on and it began to rain, Gene and I became more and more concerned. Accompanied by Johnny's mother, Pua, we went searching. Finally, we heard a faint bark, and Pua led us to the mouth of an abandoned mine shaft that Johnny had fallen into. Pua went crazy. She barked frantically as she circled the sloping entry to the vertical shaft. It was all we could do to keep her from plunging in with her daughter. When firemen pulled a dirty but otherwise dry and unhurt Johnny out of the shaft, Pua was all over her. Never a very detached mother, Pua hardly let Johnny alone for days. Although by then I'd learned to compassionately detach from clients, I couldn't help but notice the resemblance between Pua's parental attachment and my own.

In reality, compassionate detachment—even from children—is a very loving and supportive habit to cultivate. Over-attachment causes us to leap into the pit with others, whereas compassionate detachment allows us to stand on the edge of emotional and circumstantial sinkholes, hand and heart extended in understanding and support. Attachment doesn't help solve others' problems. In fact, it often adds to their discomfort by causing them to feel responsible for our feelings as well as their own. Being compassionately detached allows others to share their needs and feelings with us without worrying about overburdening us. Compassionate detachment accesses the heart energy of hope and love, while over-attachment drains our resources.

Okay, you say, compassionate detachment is excellent in theory. Now, how do we do it? By staying in the present, remembering our intention to detach, and by lifting energy to our heart centers.

A PRACTICE IN
COMPASSIONATE DETACHMENT

1. *Stay in the present.* Noted Jungian analyst Marion Woodman describes the fruits of detachment this way: "Detachment liberates the heart from the past and from the future. It gives us the freedom to be who we are, loving others for who they are. It is the leap into now, the stream of Being in which everything is possible."

Empowering the now keeps us from being overwhelmed by past and future "what if's" and "I should's" and "if only's." Being present in the moment makes it is easier to accept what is, as it is, when it is. When beset by feelings of attachment, we can ask ourselves questions such as:

- Is this current fear a reality right now?
- How are my feelings helping _____ in their situation?
- Why do I need to feel so involved with _____?

- If I could move to compassionate detachment, how might that feel?
- What can I do right now to help free myself
  and _____ by detaching?
- If there were a blessing in this situation, what
  might it be?

It's easy to slide automatically into emotional attachment
if it is a habit, our natural tendency, or because we think
it is more loving when we feel with people. Pondering the
answers to questions like those listed can help break the
bonds of over-involvement that no longer work for you
or for those whom you care about.

2. *Set and remember your intention.* Because compassionately detaching is an acquired skill, we need
   to remind ourselves of our commitment to do it.

Creating affirmations reminding us it is okay to detach
is helpful. We might affirm:

- With love and empathy, I can compassionately detach from _____'s problem with
  _____.
- I love and support _____ without being
  attached.
- I trust _____ is moving through this
  crisis constructively.

■ God is loving, holding, and guiding
_____ right now and always.

The wonder and healing power of words is not to be shortchanged. After several sleepless nights and buckets of tears, my client, Grace, is in the process of compassionately detaching from an unfair and hurtful rift between her daughter and her sister. "I just keep reminding myself that this is between Midge and Trina—not me—and that God knows the truth." With swollen eyes, but great conviction she said, "I hold onto the belief that, in the long run, this will turn out to be the best thing for both of them." As a mother, Grace is available to her daughter any time she asks and supports her with encouraging statements such as, "I know you'll come out of this an even better person." Although it's hard to become detached, Grace is helping herself do so through affirmations, crying, prayer, and talking through her feelings with friends.

3. *Lift energy to your heart center.* Attachment energy lives in the survival centers of our bodies and psyches. Compassionate detachment emanates from our hearts and souls.

Over the years my friend and mentor, Annabelle, has taught me the importance of lifting energy from the lower centers of our bodies into the center of our souls, the heart. In my imagination I liken this to adding yeast to bread in order to fluff it up and make it more delicious and palatable. Unleavened bread is heavy and hard to chew, just as energy left to fester in the lower centers of our bodies and psyches is hard to digest and can make us very uncomfortable. Interestingly, our hearts actually feel heavier when difficult energy is left hunkering in the emotional centers of the physical body: the gut and solar plexus. When we consciously lift energy into our hearts, it becomes lighter and, as a result, we experience more buoyancy and hopefulness.

Find a time when you can sit quietly for a few minutes without being disturbed. Gently close your eyes and focus on your breathing. Imagine yourself inhaling a beautiful, calming color and exhaling a disturbing or uncomfortable color. Without effort, allow your breath to deepen and slow down. Turn your attention to your body. Is a part of it calling attention to itself through discomfort? See, sense, feel, or imagine how the discomfort appears. Thank it for making itself known to you and simply focus your attention on it for a while. When it feels right, visualize moving the uncomfortable energy to your heart asking that it be transformed into the perfect, right energy in God's eyes. Keep imagining or seeing the energy moving gently into your heart where it softens, lightens, and transforms into compassionately detached love and goodwill.

When the energy is safely nested in your heart and feels as if it's transforming, even the tiniest amount, send it out to the person for whom you are concerned, including all others who may be experiencing similar difficulties. Give thanks for this experience, and focus on your breath for a few minutes before opening your eyes.

4. *Practice, practice, practice.* Like most new habits we embrace, making the art of compassionate detachment our own takes time, awareness, commitment, and practice. Practicing is well worth the effort, as compassionate detachment empowers us to be more lovingly present to ourselves and to others.

Within the freedom of compassionate detachment, we can readily care about but not carry others' burdens.

Benjamin Franklin's statement, "Dost thou love life? Then do not squander time for that is the stuff life is made of," made it clear that he understood the importance of empowering the present. Living in the moment is the best way to spend our time—our lives—wisely and powerfully. Although it might sound too good to be true, simply taking a few moments daily to fully focus on appreciation, and embracing others without internalizing their pain, really does help us find hope in the here and now.

Welcoming Heralds of Hope

Hope is the thing with feathers—
That perches in the soul—
And sings the tune without words—
And never stops—at all—
—EMILY DICKINSON

If a genie granted me three wishes, my first wish would be for a magic minute in which I could physically see the angels, fairies, guides, guardians, and other heralds of help and hope that I believe surround us all. I agree with Desmond Tutu, who says, "Angels, like parables and fine poetry, speak in many layers of meaning and mystery, trying to express the inexpressible. If we ignore them our lives are the poorer."

Although for a while Western society's love affair with all things scientific eclipsed many people's belief in the ethereal, even scientists are returning to a tentative acceptance of the efficacy of divine intervention and the possibility that there is such a thing as angelic assistance. Solar scientist Michael is a good example. Having good-naturedly pooh-poohed his wife Patsy's belief in angels for years, he's now opening to the possibility that she may be right. What is changing his mind? Cancer. Michael has returned to church after many years and is beginning to see the miraculous in both major and miniscule occurrences. Lately he has been making statements like, "It's really weird how everything seems to be falling into place . . ." and "I had the strangest feeling I wasn't alone while going through that test. . . ."

Even though his prognosis is up in the air, due to their deepening spiritual connection, Michael and Patsy are enjoying a closeness she had only dreamt was possible earlier in their relationship. "It's funny, but I really see some fabulous good coming from Michael's illness," Patsy says. "Of course, we hope and pray for remission or a cure, but it's wonderful how close we are now. I think our angels are really hard workers!"

The immediacy of illness often provides a shortcut to spiritual growth.

It doesn't matter what form our belief in the Divine takes or what we call it—Jesus, Goddess, Higher Power, Buddha, Allah, Elohim, Nature, Higher Self, Father/

Mother God, or any other name. What does matter is allowing ourselves to open to the energy of divine love and find hope in accepting the idea that God cares about our well-being and evolution.

During sharing time at our church, Anne told a story about a school for disabled children. One of the students was very frustrated because he couldn't manage his knife and fork well enough to cut his food. Instead of reaching over him or sitting beside him to help cut, a burly attendant came up behind the boy and, reaching around him, put his hands on the boy's hands and they cut his food together. The attendant was wise and kind enough to cut *with* his student rather than *for* him. Isn't that what the Divine Beloved does for us? She or He puts Her/His energy around us, embraces us, and works *with* us to help us cut through the tough stuff.

Once we understand that God is at our back ready to work with us, hope will naturally grow in our hearts.

Asking Our Angels

One of the ways we can cultivate hope and optimism is through prayer. Both scientific and empirical indicators suggest that prayer invites more hope, healing, and optimism into our lives and helps us navigate rough spots gracefully and growthfully. In one study conducted by the University of Washington Health

Sciences, researchers interviewed more than two hundred heart surgery patients, both before and after their time in the hospital. Their goal was to assess the patients' prayer practices and their feelings about the surgery and its outcome. Lead investigator Amy L. Ai, Ph.D., found that the use of prayer significantly raised a patient's optimism going into surgery. According to her report in *Research News & Opportunities in Science and Theology*, the power of prayer did not depend upon church attendance or religious preference. Interestingly, researchers did find that the effect of prayer was stronger in older patients, perhaps because they have had more opportunity to respond to and weather life crises.

To some physicians, the evidence for the healing power of prayer is simply too compelling to ignore. "I decided that not using prayer on behalf of my patients was the equivalent of withholding a needed medication or surgical procedure," says Dr. Larry Dossey, an internist and author of *Healing Words* and *Prayer Is Good Medicine*. Even the National Institutes of Health (NIH) is putting a foot on the prayer bandwagon by funding an ongoing Johns Hopkins study of women with breast cancer who say a meditative prayer twice daily.

Optimism and hope are fraternal twins.

Well-known proponent of prayer Catherine Marshall reveals, "My most spectacular answers to prayers have come when I was so helpless, so out of control as to be able to do nothing at all for myself." My friend Claudia has a life-altering brain tumor that irregularly manifests severe symptoms. After a particularly bad bout of vertigo, she had an appointment with a new woman doctor who turned out to be an unusually open and expansive physician. "We'd been chewing the fat for a few minutes," Claudia said, "when this doc says, 'Ever since you came in the office I've been wanting to tell you that you are surrounded by angels and they want me to tell you that you need to ask them for help. They need to be asked before they can do anything for you.'"

With a laugh, Claudia said, "Well, having a doctor tell me to ask my angels for help really got my attention!" Thankful for her angels' message, but still headachy and reeling with vertigo, Claudia went to bed singing the old hymn, "Blessed assurance, Jesus is mine . . ." as a gift for her angels.

During the night she awoke feeling blessed by a wonderful animal dream but disappointed that the vertigo was still present. Undeterred, Claudia sang herself back to sleep with "Blessed Assurance." She awoke the next morning singing aloud the line, "Thee who with me my burden shares . . ." from the hymn "A Closer Walk with Thee." Excitedly, she said, "The most beautiful peace surrounded me, and I felt angels everywhere gentling my soul, my symptoms, and my fears. I was totally cradled in love. I felt like a little child being rocked and sung to by the most loving mother. It was fabulous!"

Although many of us may only pray and look for evidence of angels when driven to our knees in despair, we don't have to wait until then. We can call on our angels and give wing to prayer while standing in a checkout line, between innings at a baseball game, or whenever and wherever the urge strikes us. One of my most dramatic angelic encounters happened in the dentist's office. Not the world's bravest dental patient, I prayed all the way to the office asking my angels to please be with me, protect me, and keep me from dissolving into absolute wimpdom.

Knowing my dental-avoidance difficulties, Dr. Dentist tried taking my mind off the procedure by chatting away about famous entertainment partners like Rodgers and Hammerstein. With my eyes shut (surely only dyed-in-the-wool masochists keep their eyes open while foreign objects are being stuck, pushed, and drilled into their mouths) and my sweaty hand gripping the poor dental assistant's, I was momentarily diverted into thinking about Kukla, Fran, and Ollie as a show-biz trio.

Suddenly, to the right of the dental assistant, I "saw" an angel smiling at me with great delight and unbridled affection. Never have I felt so adored, cared for, and protected. Tears of indescribable joy and elation poured out of my eyes and rolled down my cheeks. Not knowing the source of the geyser, both the dentist and his assistant instantly offered reassurance. After finally figuring out that my cotton-filled, drill-impaired mumbling had indicated I'd just seen an angel, I imagine they were even more concerned. But they were very nice about it and acted as if patients often report such sightings. Writing this, I'm both laughing and crying at the memory. At the time, I was so overwhelmed that I didn't think twice about blurting out my experience.

As "luck" would have it, I was meeting with fellow hospice chaplains that afternoon. In that safe and inviting setting, I joyfully sobbed and shared to my heart's content, and my story prompted other chaplains to reveal similar experiences. What a day! But it wasn't over. . . .

That night I was in bed thumbing through catalogs when I saw my angel! There she was masquerading as a model in a cut-rate catalog. What fun—and absolutely true to the sweetly mischievous energy I'd felt emanating from her earlier in the day. I named her Sam: S for sweet, A for adorable and adoring, and M for mischievous. Although I've never physically seen her again, I talk to her often and feel her presence regularly. Sam continues to be a welcome and valuable herald of hope in my life.

Relying on Guardians and Guides

Although angels may well assist us and intervene on our behalf more readily when we ask for help and guidance, sometimes there's no time to call out for help. Melinda, a young client of mine, was struck by lightning while riding her horse: "All of a sudden, my horse was running away, and I was filled with the worst pain imaginable. But then everything went quiet and peaceful, and the woman holding me said help was coming and I would be okay. I thought she was a hiker or something, but she disappeared when the EMTs came. I was confused when they told me I'd been alone until the man who called them ran out of his house to see if I was alive." Who knows? Maybe Melinda's heart was calling out for help without her being consciously aware of it and that was enough to bring tangible—though invisible to others— help to her. And the woman's message was true. Help came and, after physical therapy, Melinda was okay.

Asking is a choice. Intervention is a mystery.

Some people don't resonate to the idea of angels, and that's just fine. Once I was leading a young man in a guided meditation and asked him to invite into his mind's eye a wise and loving Being who cared for him unconditionally. He started laughing.

"What are you experiencing?" I asked, a little surprised at his response.

"My Being is a silly-looking squirrel with a really twitchy tail," he said.

"How do you feel about him?"

With a quiet smile, he said, "He's perfect, not very grandiose, but perfect for me."

Your herald of hope can be anything: an animal of some sort, a relative or friend who is on the other side, a sense of the Divine, or an idea that feels spiritually and emotionally right and hopeful to you. The only criterion is that your angel or herald feel loving and caring to you. As the cliché reassures us, God doesn't care what we call Him or Her, just as long as we call.

These days I've become a veritable equal opportunity asker. I'm forever imploring, thanking, and questioning whomever and whatever may be listening. My wonderful mother, who's been dead for many years, receives requests whenever my children are suffering, as do the kids' individual angels and guides.

From my first introduction to angels, the idea of Guardian Angels seemed natural, but the idea of angels as guides—or Guidian Angels, as I've come to call them—was a spontaneous gift. I was making a meditation tape for my niece who was having a mastectomy and wanted something calming to listen to before and after surgery. As usual, I asked her Guardian Angels to protect her during the procedure. Without consciously meaning to, I then requested that the medical teams' *Guidian* Angels help them access their highest professional skills and most compassionate personal selves throughout her surgery. Although I'd never used the term before—or even considered the possibility of angel as guides—the idea resonated with my heart, and I've believed in them ever since.

Guidian Angels remind me of the friends Saint Thérèse of Lisieux speaks to in the following beautiful example of asking for otherworldly assistance: "O Guardian Angel, cover me with thy wing; O Friend, illumine my path. Direct my footsteps and be my protection, *just for today.*"

*Just for today, we can give ourselves permission
to turn our hearts toward the guardians and guides
whose joy it is to assist, support, and protect us.*

Today we can embrace the beliefs that we are not alone, love is stronger than hate and ignorance, and God and good are prevailing. Today we can welcome heralds of hope into our hearts and souls by becoming aware of angelic intervention, influence, and affirmation.

Becoming Aware of
Angelic Intervention, Influence, and Affirmation

Hints of heralds are everywhere. We simply need to tune our minds and hearts and become aware of them. When you decide to buy a new car and then start seeing that kind of car everywhere; when you take up photography or painting and notice that you've started viewing everything as if it were framed; when you think of a friend with whom you haven't been in contact and then, within a few hours, she contacts you—these are all examples of magnetism and the power of focus. What we are interested in registers in our awareness. The same is true of angelic intervention, influence, and affirmation. When we set our sights on becoming aware of the whisper of angels' wings, we are likely to recognize their softly powerful touch in our lives and hearts.

Right before Christmas a couple of years ago, a voluntary screening test indicated that I had a potentially serious heart disease. Tests to confirm or refute the diagnosis—my Drama Queen personality might say "death sentence"—couldn't be scheduled until after the holidays. Not only was I afraid, I was angry and—I hate to admit it—ashamed. Shame came as a result of disparaging self-talk, much of which questioned my entire life's purpose. Was heart disease telling me that I'd failed to be loving? Had all my work centering around opening our hearts and coming from a more heart-centered space been merely a sham? Was I a fake, a phony, an imposter? Knowing it was destructive to talk to myself that way simply made me feel more like a failure. As usual, when in tough spots, I resorted to my favorite prayer: *Helpppppp!!!*

Help came in a wonderfully unique way. My sons, Mike and Brett, gave me a Zen water fountain for Christmas. It contained all the accoutrements the box promised, including a surprise bonus not listed as part of the package. Nestled in its own beautiful silk sack was a red resin figurine of a tortoise, the Chinese symbol of longevity! Ah ha . . . we chose to see that as a clever angelic affirmation that I was healthy. A weight lifted from me as we laughed and thanked whoever packed the life-affirming tortoise. After the New Year, when the cardiologist, who had done a zillion other tests, told me I had a "heart as strong as a horse," I was pleased but not really surprised.

"Tortie" was actually the second angelic intervention I experienced during the Time of Unknowing. In the midst of being bogged down in self-sabotaging thoughts and old, old patterns of behavior, I went out for a walk and fell flat-assed backward on the ice. It was the hardest fall I've taken since childhood. Miraculously—and I say that with all seriousness—I was jarred but not injured. While still on the ground, I thanked my angels and realized then and there that sometimes we can flat out fall backward into old negativity and not cause serious damage because there are guardians and guides there to cushion our falls.

Hope is an angelic attitude. It helps us see silver linings hidden within dark clouds and gives us the courage to rise above tribulation and disappointment.

Why do miracles happen at some times and not others? I don't know. We may have theoretical or heartfelt explanations, but the fact is, it's probably beyond our ability to understand. It's one of those things I keep on my list of questions to ask God after I die. For now, I'm happy to accept the Mystery and simply be thankful for each moment.

Gleaning Glimmers of Grace

I do not at all understand the mystery of
grace—only that it meets us where we are
but does not leave us where it found us.
—ANNE LAMOTT

One powerful way to grow hope is to notice and give
thanks for each tiny glimmer of grace that touches our
lives and souls. Each angelic hello, every kindness from
a stranger, every surprise smile, the love of family and
friends, every synchronicity or coincidence that brings
some sweetness into our world—these are acts of grace.
When we take less for granted and focus on those small
glimmers that, well, grace our days, we put ourselves in
a frame of mind to enjoy a deeper, richer, and wider
appreciation for what we have and who we are.

*Grace often steals into our darkest days first as an easily
dismissed, fleeting glimmer and then as a steadily increasing glow.*

Because of the trials and perils besetting our world, you
may be wondering if it is responsible or even possible to
see the grace surrounding us. With every fiber of my
being I believe the answer is an emphatic *Yes*.

As Victor Frankl said, "The last of the human freedoms is to choose one's attitude in any given set of circumstances." Herr Frankl survived Nazi concentration camp horrors and became a beloved and respected teacher who encouraged people to focus on the good around and within them. In the midst of unspeakable hardships, he was able to sustain a positive attitude, open to the reality of grace, and spread grace to his fellow prisoners. That's the way grace works. It spreads. Perhaps those of us who choose to empower the present, welcome heralds of hope, and glean glimmers of grace can become light-filled bearers of a Blessing Groundswell that brings with it an upsurge of well-being and hope. What a wonderful contribution that would be.

Seeing and Accepting Signs

This week I had a great catch-up conversation with a friend who lives many states away. We've known each other since our children were tiny babies and bonded as soul sisters while trudging through the rough terrain of divorce together. Before this talk, I'd known Pam as a person who tended to see the glass half-empty and dark clouds on every horizon. Since our previous conversation a few weeks ago, when angst and anger were roiling within her, she's changed. When asked what had shifted, she said, "These days I only let myself watch the news a few minutes a day, and I am absolutely committed to seeing the rainbows amid all the storms raging right now."

"Wow, what brought this about, Pam?" I asked.

"A couple of things. I got tired of being upset and angry all the time. I noticed my mood was negatively affecting my marriage as well as my kids and grandkids. So, I figured what the hell, I'm going to look for the good stuff!"

When I asked how the new outlook was going, she said she was feeling much better and her relationships were also lightening up and becoming fun again. And, strangely enough, she was noticing a lot more beauty and compassion around than she'd seen in a long time. "Just yesterday, I was futzing around in the yard chewing on how awful things are in the world when a butterfly landed on my hand," she said. "It was as if God was saying to me, 'Look at the beauty and delicacy I am showing you, Pam.' I took it as a sign of hope and a reminder to look for the rainbows."

Interestingly, as Pam allows herself to focus on signs of goodness and beauty, she also has more energy to be of service to people around her who need help. "Funny, how much more I have to give now that I'm not giving myself over to all the garbage that's going on."

Both miraculous and ordinary signs of benevolence

and beauty abound. It's up to us to choose to accept such signs as gifts of hope. As my friend Susan likes to say, "The reason we have seasons is to keep hope alive."

I try to remember to look around for signs of grace that I can see with my eyes and remember in my heart. The two that leap out at me right now are a vase of daffodils on the filing cabinet and a silky cat snoring on the window seat. Both warm my heart and make me smile.

Other signs of hope and grace are less obvious and up to us to interpret. While I was in the midst of an important writing project, my husband, Gene, gave me a single pink rose. It lasted longer than we could believe. On the fifteenth day—the day I'd labeled my project "cow pies on paper"—I noticed a brand new stem squashed in the narrow neck of the bud vase. The red baby leaves began to unfurl as soon as I transferred the rose to a different vase. Hmmm . . . I showed Gene the new growth on the already amazing rose, and we decided to see it as a sign that, in spite of my concern, there just might be something fresh and new lurking among the cow pies after all. Choosing to interpret the new stem as a positive sign gave me renewed energy and enthusiasm for the project.

It seems that these days more and more people are noticing miraculous signs. Stories of angelic visitations are being reported in traditional and liberal newspapers alike. Television also has a spate of shows that feature miracles and unexplained experiences, most of which have brought the recipients great peace.

I'm thankful that we can share extraordinary stories more freely now, because not feeling free to do so has caused pain for many people. One of my first hospice patients was an elderly gentleman who confided that he was pretty sure he was "cuckoo" and wouldn't be allowed into heaven. His fear was based on two experiences that had happened forty and fifty-five years before. First, his sister had appeared at the foot of his bed to tell him that she was very happy and for him not to worry about her. A few days later—news traveled much more slowly in those days—word arrived from Europe that she had died the night she appeared to him. He didn't tell anyone because he feared he was crazy.

Fifteen years later, an angel appeared to him in the boiler room of the school where he was employed as custodian. "I was so depressed that I was thinking of ending it all," my patient said. "But the angel talked me out of it." This sweet man had also kept his second amazing experience to himself. I'm so thankful he had the courage to tell me, because I was able to share similar stories other patients had told me. He was relieved to hear he wasn't the only cuckoo person around, and, with fear transformed, he died peacefully a few days later.

The way we view anything is totally up to us. We can believe in signs, miracles, and visitations . . . or not. We can see light amid darkness and despair, and we can see signs of hope everywhere. It's our choice.

Knowing our human tendency to make up stories to explain things to ourselves, I made up this motto: "If you're going to have a fantasy, make it a good one." I am supported by scholar and philosopher William James, who wrote, "Belief creates the actual fact." When we hold on to a belief in miracles, magic, and the benevolence of the Divine, it becomes a hopeful fact in our lives. Seeing and interpreting signs as one of God's ways to encourage us can give us a sense of security and bring balm to our weary souls. Plus, it's fun.

A PRACTICE FOR
NOTICING GLIMMERS OF GRACE

Just for fun, look around you right now and focus on the signs of hope and glimmers of grace. When something captures your attention, focus on it completely for a minute or so. What grace do you glean from paying close, grateful attention?

Focusing on Inner and Outer Light

One of the most beautiful things about being a human being is that, no matter how old we are or how set in our ways, we can change. We can change our minds; we can *choose* to begin anew moment to moment, day by day. We can open our heart's aperture to let in more light. We can set our intention on developing a friendly focus, one that concentrates on the good within ourselves and others rather than concentrating on fault-finding and feelings of futility. Focusing on light softens our attitudes, judgments, and fears and also helps brighten our beleaguered world. Focusing on inner and outer light encourages hope to grow.

Believe me, I know that focusing on the light in the midst of darkness is not an easy task, nor does it come naturally for many of us. But hope cannot grow in the darkness of the torment and trouble that seduce us with excitement and anxiety. At the supermarket the other day, I overheard a conversation between two women in which one was apologizing for talking about the troubles she was having. Her friend replied, "That's okay. The bad stuff is usually more interesting than the good stuff." Yikes. Hearing her remark made me wonder if our culture has developed an addiction to disaster!

If you are someone who dwells on darkness, just remember that you have the power to change your focus. At any moment. Maddie, a client of mine, has been working on her tendency to, in her words, "accentuate the negative." At a recent session she said, "I woke up this morning singing an old song from church camp days. The words are, 'This is the day that the Lord has made, let us rejoice and be glad in it.'" She went on to explain that she was surprised to be singing in the morning, because the night before she hadn't slept much due to a sinus infection. As the day wore on, it became clear that her wise subconscious had been preparing Maddie for an arduous day.

"So, the day got worse and worse with a big crisis at work and a bunch of other stuff, but I felt strangely centered and buoyant . . . that's the word! *Buoyant.* Like I could bob back up to the surface no matter what the circumstances." I asked her if she knew why she felt that way, and she answered, "I think it was pure grace. Every time I felt myself sag I noticed that a part of my brain was still singing, 'This is the day that the Lord has made, let us rejoice and be glad in it,' and a little glimmer of glad would break through."

Focusing on the light does not mean sugarcoating valid feelings and fears. As we've discussed earlier, it's important to express feelings constructively. My friend, Stacy, a very strong and capable woman, told me recently that she'd finally realized she had to find a place where she could stop being a rock and talk about her fear and anger regarding her husband's battle with cancer. As luck would have it (or was it angelic intervention?) she ran into a trusted friend who could have dinner with her on the spur of the moment. In the safety of her friend's love, Stacy was able to cry and give voice to her pent-up emotions. "Now that I've done that, I feel strong again—still mad and sad as hell—but strong enough to make it through the next step." At times, expressing darkness and despair is the only way to light a path through it.

Of course, life does not make it possible to don our Pollyanna braids all the time, nor to see light and goodness in every moment and circumstance. However, when our intention is to focus on the positive, we can learn to look for the light embedded in our feelings and circumstances, even in wrenching pain. It helps to remember that all precious gems are formed in the darkness and depths of Mother Earth, most under the onslaught of fire and extreme pressure. The same is true of many of our own precious gems, such as compassion, tolerance, creativity, faith, hope, and love. These priceless qualities are often forged in the fires of pain, disappointment, and fear.

Via letter, Marge, a reader, shared her wonderful experience of focusing on the light: "Two months ago I was blessed with cancer. I had radical breast/lymph surgery and I await chemo/radiation treatments. The waves of love, endless ways of caring that friends showered on me are totally overwhelming. I am so rich in friends, family, and angels popping in from everywhere." What priceless gems this inspiring woman must be creating in her kiln of crisis.

I love the adage, "Energy flows where attention goes," because it is absolutely true. Focusing on darkness and negativity intensifies their power over us. Focusing our attention on light and blessings energizes and empowers them and us. Have you ever noticed that you become nicer, funnier, or more creative around those people who see and relish those qualities in you? I sure have. When others acknowledge our attributes, energy flows to them and we are able to express appreciated qualities more easily and richly.

Whatever we focus on, we empower.

Right now, I'm in the process of regaining my health after being felled by a tenacious virus. Energetically, I feel like a deflated balloon. Since patience with physical ills has never been my long suit, I know I could easily do too much too soon. It's hard, but I'm choosing to give my body the positive attention it needs. I'm trying to remember to shower it with gratitude for its ability to heal, to thank it for the emotional lessons that have been part of this literal "down" time, resting it, and listening to what it needs.

A PRACTICE IN DRAWING POSITIVE ENERGY

Is there an aspect of your life that could use more positive energy? Anything meaningful to you is appropriate.

- A certain relationship?
- Taking more quiet time?
- Ways to become a better friend to yourself?
- Staying more in the present moment?
- Noticing synchronicities as possible angelic messages?
- Accentuating the positive?

When you've chosen something, try this experiment with me.

For a couple of days focus your attention primarily on the lightest and most positive facets of the aspect you've chosen. Focus on appreciation for tiny and tremendous things that are good, true, and beautiful about your chosen objective. Listen with ears tuned to understanding and a heart tuned to love. Open to the glimmers of grace flickering within yourself or the situation. Remember *energy flows where attention goes.*

By becoming aware of and acknowledging the light within ourselves, others, and life in general, we energize and empower the goodness and grace inherent within our hearts and souls. The picture I have in my mind is a fertile egg basking in the warmth of an incubator light. All toasty and cozy under the light, the chick eventually pecks free of its shell and comes to life. My bet is that there are many eggs of hope, healing, love, and creativity within you waiting to emerge from their shells when warmed by the energy of positive attention.

Letting Our Light Shine

Our deepest fear is not that we are inadequate.
Our deepest fear is that we are powerful beyond
measure. It is our light, not our darkness, that
most frightens us.
—MARIANNE WILLIAMSON

So many of us, especially girls, were taught not to "toot our own horn" or get "too big for our britches." Many of us still feel very uncomfortable if anyone compliments us in what seems too profuse a manner, or if they do so in front of others. The fear that love and approval will be withdrawn if we let our light shine too brightly still skulks around in our psyches. How unfortunate! We should be letting our light shine as brightly as it can. That's an effective way to chase away the darkness and fear that are so rampant in our families and society. If we've ever been admonished for sparkling, giving ourselves permission to shine now will take consistent commitment.

One of the ways I work with the fear that sabotages shining is simply to acknowledge it as it arises. When I find myself hastily changing the subject if someone offers a compliment, I say silently, "There you go again, Susie Q," and reassure myself that rejection or recrimination are no longer threats. I also reassure myself that what I have to contribute is valuable. It's a continuing journey.

At our grandson's birthday dinner, he asked me to read a message he'd gotten in a piece of candy. It read: "You're special just like everyone else." Hurray and halleluiah, what a sweet message to receive with a sweet. We are all special in our own unique and beautiful ways, and what a bountiful harvest of love and hope we could have if a majority of us let our lights shine for a majority of the time.

Radiating Gratitude

One of the most powerful ways to let our lights shine is to radiate gratitude. Gratitude is a warm, friendly feeling of appreciation and thankfulness. Gratitude lightens our spirits and ripens hope within our hearts like sunshine ripens wheat waving in the fields. Like any attitude, gratitude can be nurtured, cultivated, and, if need be, repotted.

> *Gratitude is the single most powerful medicine to assure physical, emotional, and spiritual health for us individually and for our planet as a whole.*

We've all experienced times when we've misplaced our sense of gratitude. Without it, doesn't the world seem to diminish and darken as if a narrow furrow of sadness, hopelessness, and negativity were closing over us? No one denies that life has its darker aspects, but we don't have to get caught up in them. When our hearts hurt and we forget to be grateful, we have to be gentle with ourselves. When I'm experiencing a forgetful time, a certain quote by thirteenth-century Sufi poet and sage Rumi helps put my gratitude-amnesia into perspective. He said, "If you put a little dab of vinegar on a mound of sugar, what does it matter?" His words softly remind me to be gentler with myself: "It's okay that you lost your attitude of gratitude for a while, Sue. It's just a dab of vinegar. If you want, you can make a different choice now. Not to worry."

Another valuable thing I've learned to do in hopeless, dark times is simply to say, "Thank you!" even when it seems phony and hollow. The intention toward gratitude and the energy inherent even in an apathetic "Thank you" seem to resonate within the very core of our being and soothe our hearts and souls. Saying "Thank you!" for something happening right now has the added bonus of returning our focus to the present and, thereby, empowering the present. For instance, at this very moment I am thankful for two distinctly different things, for the balmy breeze wafting through the window carrying with it the promise of spring and for the feelings of calm generated by my computer having one of its more cooperative days.

Sally, an attitude-of-gratitude woman extraordinaire, especially impressed me by the thoughtful and constructive way she handled a traumatic time, both for herself and her husband: "When our daughter was injured in a car accident, I was afraid my husband was going to have a nervous breakdown. I distracted him by suggesting that we make a list of things to be thankful for right now. He didn't want to do it at first, but I nagged. Actually, after we'd put together a pretty long list, including the fact that our little girl was being taken care of in a hospital, he was calmer and more optimistic." I am happy to report that their daughter is now a healthy teenager.

Even in a dire circumstance such as Sally's, there is usually something for which we can be thankful *right now*. In some moments, the basic fact that we are still breathing may be the main thing for which we can give thanks. That's okay. Anything we can say thank you for is good enough because gratitude, no matter how miniscule, opens our hearts to grace and the possibility of hope. What might you be grateful for in this very minute?

In a PBS interview, San Francisco poet and painter Lawrence Ferlinghetti said, "All I want to do is go around painting light on the walls of life." I love that image. Radiating gratitude is one of the best ways to paint light on the walls of our own and others' lives.

Practicing Gracious Acceptance

On a trip to Florida with another couple, my husband and I were beset by constant rain, relentless mosquitoes, and enervating humidity, Oh my! Luckily, Gene was reading a meditation book that included the Zen concept of *gracious acceptance*. Simply reminding each other of those two little words helped keep our spirits up, laughter flowing (not to mention the sweat), and the attitude light. Although our hopes of a sunny day were washed away, we did collect shells during lulls in the rain, and Gene and I had a great wet T-shirt, dodge-the-lightning-on-a-bicycle story with which to regale our friends. Of course we would have preferred coming home with lovely tans, but graciously accepting what was created an energy that invited a good time no matter what the weather. Railing against something we couldn't change would have dampened our spirits more effectively than rain and humidity ever could.

While many spiritual teachings urge followers to work and play with "what is" and resist floundering in "if only's," gracious acceptance is the one that resonates most resoundingly with my heart. My apologies to students of Zen Buddhism if my interpretation of the words is not in keeping with your philosophy. To me, gracious acceptance is practicing the priceless art of flexibility; bending like a reed in the face of circumstances beyond our control; adopting an openness to what is and finding the good in it. Ideally, gracious acceptance is being in a state of perpetual openness, continually able to say, "Your will, not mine" to God and believe it. Of course, no one can do that all the time, but being far from perfect in the practice of gracious acceptance shouldn't keep us from holding the *intention* to do so as often as possible.

The most important place to practice gracious acceptance is with ourselves. Not accepting ourselves is emotional abandonment—as a dear friend pointed out to me the other day after I'd spouted some shame-laden comments about myself to her. Abandoning ourselves injures our hearts, which are our chalices of hope. Having unrealistic expectations, chastising ourselves, not honoring and accepting who we are, allowing shame to roost in our hair, and judging ourselves harshly all cause tiny ruptures in our heart's energy field, out of which hope and other positive feelings can dribble away. No wonder we feel so hopeless when in the throes of self-condemnation and abandonment.

I should mention that my descent into old, icky patterns of self-recrimination was the result of being absolutely run down by a persistent illness. It's especially important to extend bottomless generosity to ourselves when we're physically or emotionally vulnerable; it supports us and invites strength and healing to return quickly.

As we treat ourselves with compassion, respect, and gracious acceptance, our hearts are encouraged to return to trust and, as a result, provide a safe haven for growing and harvesting hope.

The best model there is for gracious acceptance is water. As Chinese sage Tao Cheng states, "Water is yielding but all-conquering. Water extinguishes fire or, finding itself likely to be defeated, escapes as steam and re-forms. Water washes away Earth or, when confronted by rocks, seeks a way round." Water flows *with* the current and will find her way home even when dammed by man. Water is absolute flexibility *and* absolute strength. Given enough time, water will triumph over all other elements. No matter what the challenge or how great the odds, water stays true to her intention of returning home to rejoin her source.

A wonderfully watery one-liner in *A Course in Miracles* has been absolutely essential to my continuing cultivation of gracious acceptance. It is, *Would you rather be right, or would you rather be happy?* Before being introduced to this statement, I had always thought I would be happy if I could just be seen as right. And sometimes I was. But, if my being right meant that someone else had to be wrong, I wasn't happy at all, and neither were they. Of course, there are ideas and ideals that we must stand up for, but sometimes it's more important to stand our ground as allies, not adversaries. That makes everyone happier.

It's a continuing process—to graciously accept certain differences between ourselves and others, agree to disagree, and not label anyone as wrong or bad. But, more often than not, when I stop to ask myself which I'd rather be, I choose happy.

As we center our focus on both gratitude and accept-ance, we create a climate in which hope can flourish.

Forgiving Opens the Flow

Forgiveness is another generator of light and love. It puts us back in the flow of personal and divine love, which, of course, eventually takes us to our hearts where hope lives. By saying, "If I do not forgive everyone, I shall be untrue to myself," it seems Albert Schweitzer was suggesting that forgiveness is an authentic and integral part of being a loving and caring human being. If so, perhaps it would be accurate to paraphrase Alexander Pope's famous saying in this manner: "To err is human, to forgive divinely human."

Non-forgiveness, or being locked in an unforgiving attitude, on the other hand, creates a barrenness within us, an impassable wilderness in which we are cut off from our hearts and whomever or whatever it is we need to forgive. The energy surrounding the wound, fear, or injustice is frozen, leaving us truly "stuck" and highly susceptible to loneliness, resistance, and hope-lessness.

Withholding forgiveness actually allows another person or situation to have control over our well-being. An aphorism underscoring that fact says, "Holding a grudge is like taking poison and hoping it hurts the other person." Just as effectively as we stop water from flowing through a hose by stepping on it, hanging on to righteousness, negativity, painful feelings, and judgment puts a crimp in the flow of our life force and personal power, damming them from coursing through us. The Buddha sums this up well by saying, "When one person hates another, it is the hater who falls ill— physically, emotionally, and spiritually. When he loves, it is he who becomes whole. Hatred kills, love heals." As the Buddha knew, we need to practice forgiveness in order to open our hearts and allow God's love and our own unique life force to flow through freely.

Being human, we sometimes need to take the "low" road of righteous anger, resentment, and desire for revenge before making our way to the high road of intentionality and genuine forgiveness. It can help us forgive when we understand why someone acted in malicious and destructive ways, but understanding is often not possible. Most Westerners, for instance, find it almost impossible to fathom the motivation of suicide terrorists. To the extent that we are able to separate the action from the actor and love people with an impersonal love while absolutely abhorring their actions, we make progress on the road to forgiveness.

When forgiveness is impossible from a human perspective, we can surrender our resistance to angels and

God by sincerely asking that divine forgiveness flow through us, since we are unable to send it ourselves. Allowing forgiveness to flow *through* us rather than *from* us is perfectly all right. Having the desire to forgive is essential; the method is secondary.

If forgiveness is an issue for you, I strongly recommend you find books devoted specifically to forgiveness. *The Forgiving Self* by author Robert Karen, Ph.D. (Doubleday, 2001), is one. As well as exploring ways to cultivate forgiveness, Dr. Karen explains how research is showing that forgiving actually feels divine to those who are able to do it. According to Dr. Karen, psychological researchers have discovered that victims of abuse, as well as other emotional and physical harm, reaped many benefits from forgiving the perpetrators of their pain. Benefits are not just psychological, but also include physical health and spiritual blessings. One of the important findings in this research is that although forgiveness does bestow spiritual benefits, the act of forgiving need not be based upon any particular faith.

Allowing our light to shine, as we were created to do, shares the noble and good within us while illuminating everything and everyone around us. Empowering the present by letting light emanate from us each moment will give us the opportunity to become Blessing

Angels through whom love and grace flow. Shining the nobility of our soul's qualities and desires brightly into our personal lives and the greater global whole will help bring renewed hope, compassion, and acceptance to our own hearts as well as to our beleaguered planet, as a whole. *If not us, who?*

CHAPTER 5

SPREADING HOPE

Our hearts know
That Hope, regained, grows
                        sweeter still
When sown in
            other pastures.
—AUTHOR

In today's world, many people need a "hope infusion." As an example, this year, for the first time, Southern Methodist University in Dallas collected data regarding the reasons students sought counseling. The report stated that 54 percent of the students who wanted counseling services checked the box for "anxiety" on written intake information sheets—the highest percentage of any of the twenty-six symptoms listed. Karen Settle, SMU's director of counseling and testing, says

12 percent of the students treated at the university's mental health services have anxiety disorders, up from 7 percent last year. Ms. Settle advises those who feel anxious —young or old—to get enough sleep; eat right; exercise; do something that relaxes you; and—most important—*connect with others*. Says Settle, "Just the fact that you've reached out and they've reached back can be very helpful." Of course, the university can count only those students who *ask* for help, but there are many more of us—students, children, and adults alike— who think we should be able to single-handedly manage all pressures that come to us.

One of the best ways to grow hope in the world and retain a sense of hope within our own hearts is to extend hope to others. Sometimes even a small outreach gives a bigger boost than we can imagine. A simple smile, a sincere inquiry about another's well-being, or a short friendly e-mail may be an act of connection and compassion that brings hope to the receiver's heart. As the poem reminds us, no man or woman is an island. We are relational beings interwoven together as never before, created to count on and be of service and solace to each other. Trying to handle all things alone leads to isolation and despair. Compassionately connecting with one another cultivates healing and spreads hope.

Ours are the arms with which God hugs and holds Her children.

Spreading hope is akin to beaming rays of sunshine from the Beloved's smile upon ourselves and those we hold dear. As Aimee Semple McPherson enthuses, "O Hope! Dazzling, radiant Hope!—What a change thou bringest to the hopeless; brightening the darkened paths, and cheering the lonely way." By growing hope within ourselves and sharing it with others, we brighten darkened paths and seed lonely ways with love and positive possibilities.

Sharing the Fruits

Remember to be gentle with yourself and others. And give. Give in any way you can, of whatever you possess. To give is to love. To withhold is to wither. Care less for your harvest than how it is shared, and your life will have meaning and your heart will have peace.
—KENT NERBURN

Kent Nerburn observes that we are here to share our harvest with others, that our lives have meaning and our hearts peace when we share our bounty. Unlike an almond tree that is destined only to produce almonds, however, we human beings can choose the qualities we wish to cultivate within ourselves. We can grow love, compassion, understanding, encouragement, support, and inspiration, and share that sweet, nurturing harvest with ourselves and others. Of course, we can also drift into unconsciousness and allow the mold of cynicism, unkindness, and selfishness to taint our inner and outer harvests. But even if we do occasionally become moldy, we can always choose to turn our faces to the sun and ripen a different crop.

Well-known physician, clown, and activist Patch Adams was plagued by bouts of depression in his childhood, resulting in three hospitalizations. At a recent conference at the University of Colorado, he shared that by age eighteen he decided "never to have another bad day." Patch, who spends much of his time cheering up ill and injured children around the world and raising money for the Gesundheit Institute, a holistic medical community he founded thirty years ago, continued, "Life only has meaning if you impart meaning to it."

Patch Adams replanted himself from mental illness to the fertile field of combining clowning with doctoring and, as a result, shares healing and laughter with those who have little of either. It is also within our power to choose the fertile fields in which we can grow, ripen, and share our harvest. With commitment, intention, and perseverance, the fields of hope, happiness, and service can become ours for the pickin' and sharin', just as they are for Patch Adams.

The Sheltering Sweetness of Friendship

We are like seedlings—both strong and vulnerable—
and we must treat each other gently if we are to grow
into our full potential. That's where friends come in.
Samuel Taylor Coleridge says, "Friendship is a shel-
tering tree." As my son Mike says, "We've got to be
there for each other while we're here together." We
must be willing to shower an abundance of light and
love on ourselves and our friends while watching
patiently and enthusiastically as we slowly grow into
bearing the fruits of our hearts and souls.

These days we have solid scientific evidence that
friendship can temper stress and extend life. Shelley
Taylor, a research psychologist at the University of
California, Los Angeles, says, "Social ties are the cheap-
est medicine we've got."

Realizing that nearly 90 percent of stress research
had been done on males, Dr. Taylor and her colleague
Laura Cousin Klein, Ph.D., began to study how women
respond to stress. Whereas men release testosterone
when they are stressed, which then creates the infa-
mous "fight or flight" response, Drs. Klein and Taylor
discovered that women's bodies release the hormone
oxytocin, which buffers the "fight or flight" (if you'll
remember, in chapter 2, we added "freeze" to the standard twosome) response and encourages them to tend

children and gather with other women instead. When a woman acts on her urges and engages in this "tending or befriending," the research suggests that more oxytocin is released, which further counters stress and produces a calming effect. This "tend and befriend" ability may explain why women consistently outlive men. Countless studies have found that social ties reduce our risk of disease by lowering blood pressure, heart rate, and cholesterol. "There's no doubt," says Dr. Klein, "that friends are helping us live longer."

Interestingly, the release of oxytocin is stimulated by touch in both males and females, but oxytocin is powerless without estrogen. The fact that women naturally have more estrogen than men—sometimes a mixed blessing, to be sure—may account for oxytocin's increased production during stress. So, men, does having less estrogen to amp up oxytocin production leave you friendless and short-lived? Not at all. Biology *impels* us to act in certain ways, but it doesn't *compel* us to do so. Being aware of your natural tendency to slug it out or retreat to an isolated cave (or cubicle) empowers you to make different choices whenever you want. Whether you are a man—or a woman who has adopted the more masculine "fight, flight, or freeze" response—just for the health of it, you can *decide* to respond differently to stress and distress. You can clean the break room like

Drs. Taylor and Klein found themselves doing together when under stress; give someone a hug; share a laugh or a chocolate; or be a friend in some tangible way.

According to a 2002 *Reader's Digest* article entitled "Friends: The Secret to a Longer Life," there are many other excellent reasons to move from isolation to inclusion and connection. Author Katherine Griffin states that more than a hundred studies attest to the health benefits of friendship. People with strong social networks are shown to:

- Boost their chances of surviving life-threatening illnesses
- Have stronger, more resilient immune systems
- Improve their mental health
- Live longer than people without social support

One of my favorite studies in this area was done at Carnegie Mellon University, where they looked at the effectiveness of friendship in thwarting germs. Although I can't imagine volunteering for this test, researchers rounded up 276 volunteers, dripped cold viruses into their noses, and then quarantined them for five days. Subjects whose social networks were minimal caught a cold four times more readily than subjects who had a wide range of friends and acquaintances. I can imagine the frustrated germs assigned to multi-friended people lamenting, "Dang! This one has too many friends. I can't dig my little claws in to contaminate his system. . . ."

Friendship not only brings us better health, it is also one of our major sources of zip, zest, spice, and solace that makes life an exciting adventure rather than a test of endurance. With friends we laugh, cry, explore, and grow. By her own admission, my dear friend Bonnie is "not a good friend" in the usual sense. She doesn't answer phone calls, weeks may go by before I can track her down, and she sometimes forgets to follow through on promises. Why do I love her so and value our friendship immeasurably? Because when we do connect she is an Alka-Seltzer tablet for my heart and soul. We have a talent for "re-fizzing" each other. Plus, we laugh a lot together.

Friendship shelters us in many ways. Like the sole of a shoe, the soul of friendship eases the pain of walking through rocky times. The spirit of friendship is helium for the soul, making it possible for us to fly high and talk silly when the mood strikes. Friendship is salt, chili pepper, and sugar; it enhances the flavor of everything, spices up the mundane, and brings sweet solace to our darkest and most leaden hours.

*A true friend brings out the best
in us while knowing the worst.*

Even though privileged to our darkest fears and frail-
ties, a true friend believes in our goodness and worth,
our inherent ability to survive and thrive. A true friend
acts as a confessional in which we purge our guilt and
a kiln in which we fire our strength. However, supportive, loving friendship does not grow when
untended. As our schedules become increasingly full,
it is essential that we remember the importance of
friendship and give ourselves the life-affirming and life-
extending gift of making time for sharing the fruits of
friendship. The seeds of love in a deep and enduring
friendship need to be tenderly cared for, cultivated,
and resown.

Mirroring What Is Good,
Strong, and Beautiful in Us

One day not long ago I felt really down and called a
dear friend whom I can always count on for acceptance and support. Without preamble, I said, "Hi, it's
me, Mugsie, and I'm feeling like a pile of shit today!"
Not missing a beat, she replied, "You're the most beautiful and loving pile of shit I know." Of course her
response made me laugh, which is a wonderful first

step back into the land of self-love and acceptance. Friends like Mugs love the person you were, the one you're becoming, and the one you are right now, no matter how off-center that may be. Such friends provide a lifeline when needed *and* deepen our laugh lines on a regular basis.

Another friend of mine was cast into a crisis, not of her own making, that resulted in the loss of everything that spelled security and meaning for her entire family. Jobs, home, friends, residence in their home country: All were stripped away. After emerging from the turmoil, stronger but with an entirely new life that doesn't yet suit her as well as the former one, Gretchen said, "Others held the hope for me when I couldn't. Those who could see beyond the present circumstances and back to the capable person I had been before kept reflecting my goodness and competence to me. They acted like Plant Sitters for the Soul!"

Edith Wharton said, "There are two ways of spreading light: to be the candle or the mirror that reflects it." Keeping the faith and holding the hope for a friend—and asking for the same kind of help when we need it—encourages us all to return to hope, faith, and love and to be able to accept and act on our intrinsic positive and kind qualities.

Healing through Presence

In fact, one of the greatest gifts we can give is our accepting, open presence. It begins with the ability to be deeply present to ourselves. To acknowledge and honor our highest attributes and not abandon ourselves during occasional descents into despair—that is the surest path to feeling comfortable in being present to others even in their darkest hours. Barbara Kingsolver says, "The friend who holds your hand and says the wrong thing is made of dearer stuff than the one who stays away." I agree and also believe that fewer words make for a more healing presence.

In my private counseling practice, I've noticed that all of my clients seem to be asking for three things in relationships: "See me. Hear me. Hold me." Who among us feels we are seen clearly and compassionately, heard with patience and a sincere attempt at understanding, or held emotionally and physically as much as we'd like? And do we see, hear, and hold others as much as they want and need? I doubt many of us are completely satiated in these three vital areas. In fact, I believe our society as a whole is suffering from what I call Awareness/Attention/Affection Disorder.

A PRACTICE IN PRESENCE

The following three-step approach to Presence can help us feel more comfortable being compassionately and completely present to ourselves and others.

1. *Just sit.* In his fables, Aesop encourages us to "Give assistance not advice in crisis." Although it sounds too simple to be accurate, the best assistance we can give is our openhearted, accepting presence. Just sitting there with someone.

In my hospice training and through the patients I met there I learned so much about being present. I often didn't need to *do* anything. Simply sitting *with* someone who was dying was solace enough. I remember asking Derrick, an AIDS patient, what he would like me to do for him. He responded, "Please get me a fresh glass of water and then just sit with me. Without talking . . ." Getting the water was easy. Sitting silently became easier after I remembered a helpful hint I'd read. The author, also a hospice worker, said he found it calming for both himself and his patients if he matched his breathing to his companion's as they sat together. Breathing in harmony with someone helps us slow down and synchronize our rhythm to theirs. On occasion, breathing together can also create quite a lovely feeling of bonding.

2. *Practice attentive silence.* Compassionate, open, accepting silence is a lost art of love. Silence is a friend to the suffering, for it asks nothing while giving the blessing of presence. As Henry David Thoreau explains, "Silence is the universal refuge, . . . our inviolable asylum, where no indignity can assail."

Listening in attentive silence is one of the healing graces in friendship and humanitarian service of any kind. Through deep listening we let another know that we want to understand what they are feeling, what they want, and what is important to them. Understanding and empathy naturally grow out of hearing into the heart of another person. Since *listen* and *silent* contain exactly the same letters, maybe the creators of the English language were trying to emphasize the importance of closing our mouths and opening our ears.

On the other hand, sometimes a few soft mothering murmurs can be the key to opening the cleansing floodgates. I was holding my friend, Sarah, who was stoically avoiding crying even though she had just learned her best friend had died in an accident. I rocked her a little and murmured the same "ooos" and "ahhhs" I would have used with an injured or frightened child. It wasn't long before healing tears began to flow. (Tears actually *are* healing! Research has shown that tears of joy and awe do not contain toxins, while tears of grief, pain, frustration, and depression are chock full of poisons.)

3. *Be a feeling sieve.* Sometimes the best thing we can do for another is to be their feeling sieve. What in the world do I mean? We all know the importance of taking out the garbage and the consequences that inevitably occur if we let it pile up inside the house. The same is true of many feelings. Not getting them out of our bodies and minds will eventually create a big stink. Often the best way to release potentially putrid feelings is to express them to someone who we know can *hear* but not *hold* them. Feelings are fleeting and always subject to change. Because of the transitory nature of feelings, we need to entrust them to people who will not cast them in cement but can receive them in a compassionate sieve.

Recently I received an especially long e-mail from an old, old friend who prefaced it by saying, "I just needed to get all this stuff out and I knew you could hear it and let it go! So here goes. . . ." She then poured her hopelessness, rage, and garbagey feelings into the computer. I read them, wrote back briefly to commiserate, and quickly deleted the message. In other words, I performed a sieving service for Patti.

Some feelings, like Patti's, are more easily sieved than others. If we are caught in the middle of a family squabble, for instance, it can be close to impossible to sieve those feelings. Sieving is only healing when we can do it wholeheartedly, without damaging or over-burdening ourselves as a result. Therefore, it is crucial that we be honest with ourselves, as "dumpee," and also with "dumpers" about whether or not we can easily release their feelings and not be contaminated in the process. Sieving is good, cementing is not.

Both bestowing and basking in the healing gift of Presence is a balm beyond compare. Seeing and being seen, hearing and being heard, and holding and being held within the embrace of loving acceptance encourage seeds of hope and healing to bloom in our hearts, souls, and bodies.

Souls of a Feather

In the *Iliad*, Homer tells us, "God always pairs off like with like." Finding a community of people in which to feel nested gives us a solid and trustworthy foundation from which to fly to ever-higher realms within ourselves. Just as tennis students are encouraged to improve their games by playing with partners and opponents who are more experienced than they, we are wise to choose souls of a feather who inspire us to consider new ideas and challenge us to open up to new heights within ourselves. And we can return the favor. As we stretch and grow, hope grows within us.

While some of us thrive on being in unfamiliar territory and use excursions into the unknown to grow and change, others find it easier to grow hope and find the courage to live authentically in the security of being with like-minded and like-hearted people. No matter our bent, it's important that we be able to share who we really are, what we've experienced, and how we cope and celebrate in our lives.

Supported, we fly. Isolated, we wither and die. As Desiderata tells us, "Be yourself. Especially do not feign affection. Neither be cynical about love; for in the face of all aridity and disenchantment it is as perennial as the grass." Gather with individuals and groups with whom you can be yourself. Listen as they encourage you to love yourself as is *and* grow beyond current limitations into the light of your true Self. Seek out those for whom you can do the same.

Go where hope is nurtured. *Be* a consciously hopeful person. *Share* hope with others.

Expanding the Circle

Almost anything you do seems insignificant.
It is very important that you do it. You must be
the change you wish to see in the world.
—MAHATMA GANDHI

One day while driving and thinking about Gandhi and the idea of oneness—which is not a slam-dunk, yes-I-*get*-it idea for me—I envisioned the human family as an old-fashioned fishing net. It came to me that our individual efforts could be likened to the knots holding the strands of netting together into a functional whole. If we don't tie the knots given us, no matter how miniscule we may think they are, a link will be missing and a hole will be created in the net. As each of us does his share of light bearing and knot tying, the entire net becomes strong and capable of casting a wider circle and pulling in a more abundant harvest.

There is a wonderful story from the Sufi tradition that highlights our individual responsibility to be the change we hope for in our personal worlds as well as the greater whole. A holy woman was sitting outside the temple watching a tide of people pass. To her they represented a river of hopeless need. Among the passersby were the crippled and wounded, the drunk and dastardly, the lonesome and outcast. During her prayers, she cried out to God, "How can a loving creator see such suffering and not do something to help?" And God answered, "I did do something. I made you."

As God's doers incarnate, we can expand the circle of humanitarianism by growing hope and peace within our own hearts and, through our attitudes and actions, allow it to be an inspiration for hope and peace throughout the world. We, too, can be light bearers for faith, hope, and love. Not all the time, of course, but enough of the time to make a big difference.

Giving Is Beneficial to All

Aubrey Verboven, a Doctors Without Borders volunteer, said in a recent magazine interview, "As we drive back from the hospitals, children jump up and down and wave to us. For a fleeting moment I forget the war and know there is still hope." For these doctors, nurses, and other volunteers, giving in the face of extreme hardships and under horrific circumstances fills their hearts with love and hope and certainly brings much-needed help to those who require medical services. Such admirable actions are good for both giver and getter.

While it may be true that people who need other people are lucky, new evidence has found that the luckiest people are actually the ones whom needy people need. The University of Michigan's Institute for Social Research conducted a five-year study of 423 couples over the age of sixty-five. Researchers discovered that those who were looking out for someone else—either by providing emotional help to a spouse or tangible help to a person in another household—were about half as likely to die as those who did neither. Interestingly, they discovered that, for those on the receiving end, getting help didn't seem to affect survival one way or the other. However, if needy people receive what they need, it seems logical to me that finding a need and filling it is a win-win situation for everyone involved.

Even if you never go to a Third World country or become a caregiver to a loved one, you can be of service wherever you are, even comfortably seated on your couch. One way to do that is to give money to the countless organizations and causes that need our help and resonate with our hearts. Another is by praying. Prayer is a gift that has a double blessing, because you can't pray for someone else without feeling the uplifting effect in your own heart, mind, and life. Taking others into the circle of our arms through hugging and holding and into the circle of our compassion by listening and trying to understand them are both invaluable services.

Our form of service is unimportant; it is doing what we can, where we can, when we can that is essential and beneficial. During World War II, a Dutch girl named Corrie ten Boom and her parents were imprisoned for helping Jewish people escape the Nazis. In spite of the fact that Corrie suffered great hardship for being helpful, she has a playfully profound philosophy regarding service. She says, "If you are unhappy with your lot in life, build a service station on it."

Inspiring through Attitude and Action

When asked what his religion is, His Holiness the Dalai Lama responds, "My religion is kindness." With kindness as his modus operandi, the Dalai Lama spends his life as an inspiration to all whom he meets. I have seen him in person, and he absolutely radiates happiness and humor. Obviously, being deeply committed to kindness has been beneficial for him as well as those who hear him speak and read his books. But, you might be saying, the Dalai Lama is a holy man, a very evolved soul. What about unkind people and disrespectful kids? Yes, there are people of all ages who cast dark shadows in the world and there are many more who carry and spread light, young people included.

I found a very hopeful example in an article by a senior in high school whose life has been dramatically complicated due to persistent symptoms of Obsessive Compulsive Disorder, an imbalance in brain chemistry that is difficult to treat and even more difficult to live with. Nonetheless, Andy, a thoughtful and caring young man, wrote the following:

Saving the World with Kindness

Giving is much better than receiving. Anyone can sit around getting stuff, but it takes a good-hearted person to spend their time giving to others. There is really no reason that anyone cannot take some time out of their day to make someone else's day better. Mean and selfish people just are not very helpful when it comes to building a more caring society. So if you fall in this category, do the right thing and change. Relationships and giving to others should be number one on everybody's priority list. Learn to be selfless.

Worry more about what you are than what you own.

Even in the face of extreme anxiety and uncertainty, Andy has chosen kindness as his life's strategy. Andy's peers have responded to him in kind by appreciating his writings and electing him to this year's Royal Homecoming Court.

The point is, no matter what the situation, we always have the power to choose to spread the fruits of love, hope, and kindness. We can live love—or any other quality—one choice at a time. In the 1950s, a Ban-the-Bomb activist named A. J. Muste stood on street corners with placards and preached against war and weapons. When asked by a reporter why he did this when no one paid any attention, Muste answered, "I'm not doing this to change the world; I'm doing this to keep the world from changing me."

Take a moment now to ask yourself if the negativity in the world is pulling you from your center or from the integrity of your Soul Self. If so, what thoughts and attitudes need to be transformed in order for you to act from the goodness and kindness of your authentic Self?

Physician and clown Patch Adams asks two questions in his four-hour intake interview with new patients: "What do you want?" and "What are you doing to get there?"

What do you want? What might you do to increase the amount of hope, health, and happiness in yourself and in the world? Whatever you really want to do, I truly believe you can do it. Go for it!

Becoming an Emissary or an Eeyore

We can dance through life's gardens scattering seeds capable of blooming into beautiful flowers of love, or we can sit among the blossoms planted by others and, with a sigh, dismiss the loss of our tails by saying, "It wasn't much of a tail anyway!" as Winnie the Pooh's friend, Eeyore, has been known to do. Of course, it's perfectly understandable to have an occasional Eeyore day when our emotional tails are tucked between our legs, if not lost altogether. Habitually living in Eeyore Land, however, is detrimental to your peace of mind and quickly drains reservoirs of hope.

Actually, I never cease to be awed by the way most people creatively adapt to and embrace the vicissitudes of life. Lily, whose husband is fading away from an undiagnosed illness, smiled through her tears as she told Gene and me, "I don't expect him to live through the year, but we're so thankful for the time we've had together. We make every minute count. He is my Earth Angel, and I'm so grateful to have been able to share my life with him for a few years."

Through her acceptance of what is and gratitude for what has been and will be for a while longer, Lily is an everyday emissary of hope, acceptance, and silver-lining-looking. Dr. Rachel Naomi Remen, author of *Kitchen Table Wisdom*, points out our ability to be healing presences to each other: "We heal each other all the time, and don't even realize we're doing it. We're all wounded. People who have lived life with any depth or taken any necessary risks in life have experienced loss and disappointment. The experience of being wounded, and what happens to one as one responds to the wound, give us the wisdom to heal one another."

Whether they realize it or not, people like Lily, who glean wisdom and compassion from pain, become inspirations to others. By desiring to be of service, growing hope in our own hearts, and sharing the fruits of friendship, we, too, can expand the circle of brothers and sisters for whom hope, healing, and happiness are a reality. As emissaries of hope, we can choose to spread love and instill optimism one thought, one sentence, one smile, one act, one relationship at a time.

> May peace live in your heart
> May hope lift your spirit
> May love be your guiding light.

CHAPTER 6

WATERING SEEDS OF HOPE

Only when nurtured
                by the
                        life-giving
Waters of
           conscious care and
                      compassionate attention
Will hope remain
                alive
In our hearts.

—AUTHOR

This final chapter is comprised of quotes, poems, proverbs, and aphorisms that can help us nurture, cultivate, and grow hope until it spreads over all the planet. The creators—wise, kind, creative, and spirit-filled people—are forging a path in consciousness for us to follow. They are our angels of inspiration, tweaking our minds with new ideas, instilling hope in our hearts, and encouraging our souls to sing their unique songs. Following the quotes are simple activities, ideas, or meditations designed to water the seeds of hope within your heart, mind, and soul. Let your intuition and wisdom lead you to the thoughts and activities that resonate with your heart. And, most of all, enjoy yourself!

Thoughts on Love and Inspiration

A friend may well be reckoned the masterpiece of Nature.
—RALPH WALDO EMERSON

Those friends thou hast, and their adoption tried,
Grapple them to thy soul with hoops of steel.
—WILLIAM SHAKESPEARE

Cultivate. Reach out. Call, write, visit, or e-mail a friend and tell them what blessings and joy they bring to your life. Give them a written, verbal, or physical hug.

Treat people as if they were what they ought to be and you help them become what they are capable of being.
—JOHANN WOLFGANG VON GOETHE

Cultivate. Gaze at yourself, a family member, or a friend as if you are looking through the eyes of God. See them—and yourself—as perfect, whole, and wise. Pick a positive quality alive in their lives and actions and mirror it back to them through appreciation and affirmation. Remember to do the same for yourself. . . .

⁓

Born of my heart, our bloodline is spirit.
—ANNABELLE K. WOODARD

Cultivate. Make a mental or written list of members of your "chosen family" for whom you are grateful. Buy or make a card to my "mother, sister, brother, father . . ." and let them know how thankful you are to be a part of their spirit-family.

It's also fun to do a "choosing" ritual of adoption or commitment with a like-hearted friend. I have two chosen sisters with whom I have done such a ceremony. For us, it made a meaningful difference.

⁓

The words of the tongue should have three gatekeepers.

- Is it true?
- Is it kind?
- Is it necessary?

—ARAB PROVERB

Cultivate. Today, speak from the heart of love; say only that which is kind, true, and appropriate.

~

The soul is awakened through service.

—ERICA JONG

Cultivate. Do at least two small acts of service for two different people this week. It can be something as simple as throwing your neighbor's paper closer to their door.

~

Kind words can be short and easy to speak, but their echoes are truly endless.
—MOTHER TERESA

Cultivate. If you remember kind words that have echoed down the corridors of your life, thank the person who said them. If the person is dead, or otherwise unavailable, say a little prayer of thanks and ask their angels to wing the energy of your gratitude to them wherever they are.

Say a few kind words to someone whose path you cross this week.

∽

No matter what the question, love is the answer.
—AUTHOR

Contemplate. Sit quietly for a moment and focus on your breath. Gently observe your life-giving breath moving in and out of your body. Allow a question that concerns you to come to your awareness. If you were to address this question solely from a loving perspective, how might that change the answer or the question itself?

∽

O, heavenly Father, protect and bless all things that have breath; guard them from all evil, and let them sleep in peace.
—ALBERT SCHWEITZER

Cultivate. Say this prayer for all breathing beings before sleeping, and think of three people whose names you can insert. Repeat the prayer for each one of them every day for a week. Intercessory prayer is a loving gift all of us can give.

~

I hold to my ideals because, in spite of everything, I still believe that people are really good at heart.
—ANNE FRANK

Contemplate. Think of Anne Frank, and other angels of inspiration, who maintained a positive attitude in the face of tragedy and turmoil, and offer a little prayer of thanks for the light they brought or bring to our world.

~

An idea, in the highest sense of that word, cannot be
conveyed but by a symbol.
—SAMUEL TAYLOR COLERIDGE

Cultivate. Create a sacred space in your home or office; an
altar, sand tray, or shelf will do nicely. Place objects that
are symbolic of soul and spirituality to you in the space.
Symbolism strums our heartstrings and helps remind us
of the Selves we really are.

As I think of God's light, I picture the inviting glow of a
lantern. Although its glow can light only the area
immediately around it, I know that as I carry a lantern
with me, it continues to illumine my path.
—UNITY LENTEN BOOKLET, 2003

Contemplate. I keep a tall votive candle lighted at all times.
It reminds me to pray for the people whose names are in
the prayer box beside it. The flickering candlelight also
acts as a beacon of hope and promise if I awaken in the
middle of the night with the darkness of confusion or
sadness shrouding my heart.

We are all born to be a blessing.

—RACHEL NAOMI REMEN

Contemplate. Without false humility, think of ways others may see you as a blessing. Allow yourself to honor and appreciate the ways in which you bless others and, consequently, encourage them to hope.

Bidden or not bidden, God is present.

—CARL G. JUNG

Contemplate. Look for God in the center of a flower, the whiskers of a cat, the giggle of a child, the pain of a loss, the beauty of a sunset, or the heroics of a search-and-rescue team.

Thoughts on
Self-Care and Creativity

Self-love is not only necessary and good, it is a
prerequisite for loving others.
—ROLLO MAY

Cultivate. Sit quietly with your eyes closed for a moment
while effortlessly concentrating on your breathing. Silently
ask yourself what you might do for yourself today that
would be loving and supportive. Listen attentively, and take
at least a small step toward fulfilling your inner Self's request.

It is not possible for the human mind to hold both a
positive and a negative thought at the same time.
—LILY TOMLIN

Cultivate. Today, when you notice negative weedlike
thoughts crowding out the positives in your mind, replace
them with hopeful flowerlike thoughts.

Life is a paradise for those who love many things with a passion.
—LEO BUSCAGLIA

Cultivate. Choose one thing you love with a passion and indulge in it for 10 minutes today or tomorrow.

⁓

Row, row, row your boat gently down the stream....
—CHILDREN'S NURSERY RHYME

Contemplate. Decide on one way in which you will stop battling the current and, instead, float gently downstream with the flow. Perhaps you will give up a power struggle with a boss, employee, or child. Maybe you will accept and revel in weather conditions that change your plans. Or possibly you will stop working and sit as soon as you're tired rather than forcing yourself to keep on keepin' on even though your eyes are drooping and your body yearns to rest.

⁓

In times of darkness
                    and despair
Hope nudges doubt
                    aside
And, like a tiny breeze,
Fans the embers
                    in my heart

—AUTHOR

Cultivate. Sit in the warmth of the sun—or the glow of a lamp or candle—and put your hands over your heart. Invite any fear trembling there to make itself known to you; reassure it of the safety of revealing itself. Allow a picture of the fear to come into your mind's eye. Imagine a soft breeze blowing away any cloud cover, and feel the light of the sun warming and softening the fear. Increase the warmth and brightness of the light, and invite the fear to use the light to transform into the perfect, right energy. Thank yourself for doing the exercise, no matter what turns it may have taken.

We could never learn to be brave and patient if there were only joy in the world.

—HELEN KELLER

Contemplate. Think of one sorrow that has brought you courage and patience, and give thanks for it and the growth it provided.

Hope begins in the dark, the stubborn hope that if you just show up and try to do the right thing, the dawn will come. You wait and watch and work: you don't give up.

—ANNE LAMOTT

Cultivate. Give yourself praise and recognition for the times of darkness you weathered, the dawns you waited for, and the courage it took not to give up. With the wisdom and compassion born of experience, be present to someone who is currently waiting for their dawn to come.

Tapping into our creativity is inviting the energy of the Creator and Creatress to flow through us.

—AUTHOR

Cultivate. Ask yourself, What do I love to create? Gardens, cookies, works of art, birthday cakes, sewing or stitching projects, a tidy spreadsheet, an inviting, welcoming home? A friend of mine calls puttering around her house; trimming plants, organizing the spice rack, arranging flowers, and beautifying her home "making love to my house." Spend a few minutes today making love to yourself by being creative.

I did not write it. God wrote it.
I merely did his dictation.
—HARRIET BEECHER STOWE (REFERRING TO UNCLE TOM'S CABIN)

Cultivate. Find a time when you will not be disturbed for a few minutes. With a pen and pad of paper nearby, quiet your mind and heart by closing your eyes and breathing slowly and rhythmically. Effortlessly allow your breath to deepen and your body to relax. Invite your personal Muse to sit beside you as you write whatever comes into your mind and heart. Without judgment, allow your mind to wander and your hand to write the wanderings. There is no right or wrong way to do this exercise. It is simply opening the door a crack to allow the flow of creative energy through. When we first start going with the flow in writing, much of what we write will be gibberish. That's perfectly okay. It can even be fun. The trick is to keep inviting your Muse to express herself.

When the poet in each of us dies, God is strangled.
—W. PAUL JONES

Cultivate. While the previous writing exercise was very free-flowing, this one is structured. Try your hand at writing a haiku poem. A haiku poem has three lines. The first line consists of five syllables, the second line has seven syllables, and the third line has five. The theme of a haiku usually has at least a hint of nature in it. I wrote the following haiku about the differences in our family members' views on religion and spirituality:

Wolves together stand
Howling soft and loud at light,
Singing family songs.

(You can see the Missouri background in my two-syllable pronunciation of family. . . .)

Try it. It's fun and gets the creative juices flowing.

This is what I want from now on: a slower pace, a more centered existence, and the feelings of perfect happiness to be found in the moments I come home to myself.

—LINDA WELTNER

Cultivate. Ask yourself:

1. What and where is home to me? Both my inner and outer homes.

2. How often do I come home to myself?

3. What small step can I take today to make sure I come home to myself as often as is optimal for my peace of mind and hopefulness?

Silence lets the one behind your eyes talk.

—RUMI

Contemplate. Make a commitment to step outside the rushing current of your life for 10 minutes each day to silently listen to the one who lives behind your eyes: the still, small voice of your higher Self.

Thoughts on Surrender and Trust

Falling in the Future Hole drains hope from our hearts in the blink of a fear.

—AUTHOR

For peace of mind, resign as general manager of the universe.

—LARRY EISENBERG

Cultivate. Write one fear you have about the future on a slip of paper, burn it, and scatter the ashes to the wind or bury in a flower pot. Ask your Guardian and Guidian Angels to take over managing this particular concern.

How do we grieve? Awkwardly. Imperfectly. Usually with a great deal of resistance. Ultimately, by surrendering to the pain.
—UNKNOWN

Contemplate. If you are experiencing a river of grief right now, through visualization, writing, or talking with a friend or therapist explore the river metaphor. How deep, how wide, how turbulent, how strong is the current in this river? Ask your wise Higher Consciousness to show you the perfect, right boat for your journey. A beautiful craft: safe, sturdy, able to right itself through all types of undertows and tides. Imagine the companions—both inner and outer—whom you would like to travel with you.

Cultivate. During times when it seems almost impossible to remain afloat, remember your beautiful, safe boat and the beings who are traveling with you. Ask them for comfort, strength, reassurance, and whatever else you may need. Surrender to their care and rest in their embrace.

Grief is a process. If it is allowed, healing takes place naturally.

—HOSPICE OF NEVADA COUNTY

Contemplate. We run from grief because we fear we'll be consumed by it if we open the door to our true feelings. The opposite is actually true. When denied, grief can freeze us into a walking iceberg in order to protect us from vulnerability. Surrendering to the pain and grace of grief allows us to heal day by day, increment by tiny increment. Eventually we will be strong enough to think about creating a new kind of life. A life without our loved one but a meaningful one, nonetheless.

Cultivate. If you are grieving, please find the support you need to naturally move through the painful process into the grace of healing.

Writing is a form of release that washes the soul and warms the heart.

—AUTHOR

Cultivate. When feeling resistant—or any uncomfortable or limiting feeling—try writing a paragraph or poem without censor. Simply allow the words to flow. After writing, ask, "Who wrote this?" So often we try to avoid the aspects of our selves that have ugly traits, but they need loving, too. Next inquire, "What do you want and need?" To the best of your ability, give them what they crave. My Drama Queen wanted a sympathetic but lighthearted audience. At the finale of her oh-so-dramatic soliloquy, she received a standing ovation from the audience I rounded up. It was fun, and the laughter that followed washed away resentment, resistance, and my foul mood.

Sorrow is such a faithful guide.

—JAN ESHER

Contemplate. Gently allow yourself to remember a time (it may be right now) when your heart was leaden with sorrow. What growth or blessing have you been led toward as a result of the pain? Take a moment or two to feel gratitude for Sorrow's guidance.

When we avoid being vulnerable, we invest our energy in defenses.
—JACK SCHWARZ

Contemplate. A Course in Miracles states, "In my defenselessness, my safety lies." The next time you find yourself building defenses, pause, take a few deep breaths, and ask what vulnerability lies beneath "de fence" you are constructing. Love, nurture, and hold your vulnerable self while letting defenses fall.

If the deck is stacked against you, stop playing.
—UNKNOWN

Cultivate. No matter how hard we try, there are some games we can't win and people we can't win over. If you're embroiled in a lose-lose situation, stop playing. Fold up the losing hand, and let go of the chronic frustration or sadness. Give the situation to God and be free.

Turn thy face to the light and the Shadows fall behind.
—EDGAR CAYCE

Cultivate. Worrying means we've lost sight of faith and trust. In whom or what do you trust? Consciously turn your face to the source of light most meaningful to you and ask that it/they take care of the source of your worry. Friends can help turn us toward the light of trust. If I'm worried about one of my children, for instance, my friend Judith will remind me that they are in God's care and that their souls are perfect and whole no matter what may appear to be true on this earth plane. Judith helps me turn to the light within myself, which allows the shadows to fall behind me and encourages trust and hope to return to my heart.

Do not feel totally, personally, irrevocably,
responsible for everything. That's my job.
Love, God
—UNKNOWN

Contemplate. Consciously let go of one responsibility that really isn't yours to handle. Say "No," plain and simple.

Sad soul, take comfort, nor forget
That sunrise never failed us yet.

—CELIA THAXTER

Cultivate. On a sleepless, restless night, stay awake on purpose to watch sunrise come and invite the hope of perpetual sunrise to rise in your heart and soul.

~

The most important of all the virtues is courage, because without courage you can't practice any other virtue with consistency.

—MAYA ANGELOU

Hope resides in the center
Of a soft, yet courageous, heart.

—AUTHOR

Cultivate. Name and claim at least one courageous change in attitude, action, or reaction you've made within the last few months. Congratulate yourself on your courage then, and consciously choose to trust that the same courage is within you whenever needed.

~

And all will be well. And all manner of things will be well.
—SAINT TERESA OF AVILA

Cultivate. Repeat, sing, chant, or silently affirm Saint Teresa's beautiful reassurance whenever negative or fearful thoughts disturb your peace of mind.

～

There is nothing
which heaven does not
cover,
and nothing which earth
does not
sustain.
—CHUANG TZU (369–286 B.C)

Contemplate. Choose to trust in the truth of Chuang Tzu's message, and hope will grow unhindered.

Thoughts on Acceptance and Forgiveness

You have to accept whatever comes, and the only important thing is that you meet it with the best you have to give.

—ELEANOR ROOSEVELT

Contemplate. Sometimes the best we have to give is the hope we will somehow survive. Accepting our feelings, whatever they are, better prepares us to courageously meet what comes and eventually glean compassion and wisdom from the experience

Seeing the small
is called Clarity.
Keeping flexible
is called Strength.

—LAO-TZU

Contemplate. The flexibility of the willow ensures it will remain strong and whole no matter how harsh the wind. The flexibility gained from graciously accepting circumstances gives us the strength to remain upright and hopeful during both calm and chaos.

Many of life's gifts seem to come in tattered wrappings.
—AUTHOR

Contemplate. Look back at one or two of life's blessings that seemed a lot more like garbage than gifts when they arrived. What surprising gifts were a result of those tattered and tearing experiences? (I think of the self-esteem and new life's direction that emerged from the pain of divorce.)

Cultivate. Are there loose ends to tie up from those gifts in tattered wrappings? Remnants of thankfulness left to express or people still needing to be forgiven? If so, complete the package.

Where there are humans
You will find flies
And Buddhas.
—KORBAYASHI ISSA

Contemplate. When an irritating person buzzes around you, imagine they are a camouflaged Christ or Buddha.

Fire destroys that which feeds it.
—SIMONE WEIL

Contemplate. Thinking about the wrongs done to you and the people who did them stokes the fires of anger, resentment, fear, and hopelessness. Ask that the spirit of forgiveness wash away feelings holding you hostage. Cleanse your heart, mind, and spirit to receive feelings, attitudes, and beliefs that bring you love, hope, and joy. Open to freeing yourself through forgiving others.

~

To be wronged is nothing unless you continue to remember it.
—CONFUCIUS

You can focus on what somebody did and be in hell or you can overlook it.
—MARIANNE WILLIAMSON

Contemplate. Obsessing about another's behavior is an exercise in agony and impotence. We can do nothing about what they did, or are doing, but we can do everything about the focus of our own attention. Turn the channel of your mind away from upsetting thoughts and focus, instead, on those people and things that lift you up and lighten your outlook.

Thoughts on Gratitude and Joy

Keep a grateful journal. Every night, list five things that you are grateful for. What it will do is change your perspective of your day and your life.
—OPRAH WINFREY

Cultivate. 'Nuff said. . . .

~

Ten thousand flowers in spring, the moon in autumn, a cool breeze in summer, snow in winter. If your mind isn't clouded by unnecessary things, this is the best season of your life.
—WU-MEN (ANCIENT CHINESE SAGE)

Contemplate. What is the most priceless thing about this season of your life? Allow your mind to quiet and clear like an alpine lake after a storm has passed, and spend a few moments looking into its depths to appreciate and give thanks for this season's most priceless gifts.

~

Blessed are those who can give without remembering
and take without forgetting.
—ELIZABETH BIBESCO

Cultivate. Do one anonymous good deed each week. We
all say habitual thank you's each day, and they are nice
and polite. Today, however, give someone a heartfelt and
conscious "Thank you" for something received, complete
with eye contact and a sincere smile.

He who binds to himself a joy
Does the winged life destroy;
But he who kisses the joy as it flies
Lives in eternity's sunrise.
—WILLIAM BLAKE

Contemplate. Before getting out of bed tomorrow—and
any morning you can remember to—make a commitment
to notice and kiss the joys that fly by today.

Joy is what happens to us when we allow ourselves to recognize how good things really are.
—MARIANNE WILLIAMSON

Cultivate. Think of at least three things that are really good right now in yourself, your family, among your friends, and in the world. Celebrate them with a piece of chocolate, a song of gratitude, a prayer, or a whoop and a holler.

We make a living by what we get, we make a life by what we give.
—SIR WINSTON CHURCHILL

Cultivate. Give your life a lift by being of service in a small or major way today.

Our consciousness can be described as soil, containing many seeds of joy and suffering. It is important to touch the seeds of joy within yourself, to water them every day. And we can ask someone we love: "Please refrain from watering the seeds of anger and despair in me. Instead, please recognize and water the seeds of joy and peace." This is a very important practice of love.

—THICH NHAT HANH

Cultivate. Conspire with a loved one to create a beautiful garden by watering the seeds of hope and joy within each other. Use a watering can filled to the brim with love.

What a wonderful life I've had! I only wish I'd realized it sooner.

—COLETTE

Cultivate: Make a mental or written list of wonders and joys you may have missed in the past, and rejoice in them now. Instead of counting sheep to fall asleep, acknowledge all the wonderful things that happened to you and within you this day. Appreciating each day makes for a wonderful life!

Thoughts on Hope
and the Here and Now

Happiness is a present attitude—not a future condition.

—HUGH PRATHER

Contemplate. Take a moment to check your attitude right now. If you are harboring a belief that "I'll be happy as soon as . . . or if thus and so happens . . . ," turn your attention to the present. What can you feel happy about right now?

Now or never! You must live in the present, launch yourself on every wave, find your eternity in each moment.

—HENRY DAVID THOREAU

Contemplate. It is said that one drop of water contains the entire ocean. Ask yourself, What tiny miracle can I focus on that brings eternity to this moment in my life?

You don't get to choose how you're going to die. Or when. You can only decide how you're going to live. Now.

—JOAN BAEZ

Contemplate. If you knew you were going to live only a few tomorrows, what would you change today?

◦

Each beautiful flower, each bountiful fruit is present in the seeds of today.

—AUTHOR

Contemplate. In the expression of our whole and healthy selves, hope grows abundantly. In quiet and solitude, muse about the seeds waiting within you yearning to bear fruit and blossom. What creativity wishes to express itself, what service desires to be given, what attitude longs to reflect the beauty of your soul?

◦

You want nothing but patience—or give it a more fascinating name, call it hope.

—JANE AUSTEN

Cultivate. What pockets of positivism instill hope and patience in your heart? A certain place in Mother Nature's beauty? A friend, group of friends, or a community endeavor? Think of hopeful and optimistic people, places, and activities. Visit one within the week. For instance, you may want to drop by a playground and watch children in their innocence and joy. You know what feeds your heart and soul. . . . Give yourself a banquet!

Hope, like the gleaming taper's light,
Adorns and cheers our way;
And still, as darker grows the night,
Emits a brighter ray.

—OLIVER GOLDSMITH

Cultivate. Consciously send a ray of hope and love to someone whose heart is hurting. Imagine the warmth of your concern penetrating their sadness and bringing a small increment of peace to their day.

The first hope in our inventory—the hope that includes and at the same time transcends all others— must be the hope that love is going to have the last word.

—ARNOLD J. TOYNBEE

To ensure that love has the last word in our world, it must bloom in each individual heart. Today, we can do our part by valuing life, walking in peace, and living in love. Our sacred purpose and joy are to open our hearts in an ever-increasing capacity for love and to pour that love and compassion upon ourselves, our circle of family and friends, and the greater community. By sowing the seeds of positive change in ourselves and the world, we create an environment in which hope—and all that is good, true, and beautiful—can flourish.

In closing, let me send you off with a blessing to encourage your heart to bloom with hope.

Blessed are those who cultivate . . .
· Gentleness
Live gently with yourself and others.
· Gratitude
Gratitude is grace; God's energy within us.
· Generosity
Extend bottomless generosity and forgiveness to those
who baffle you.
Including yourself.
· Gracious Acceptance
Gracious acceptance gives us strength and flexibility and oils the apparatus of life.
· Giggles
Laughter lightens even the darkest corners
for they shall have Hope.

About the Author

 Sue Patton Thoele is a therapist and author of ten books, including *The Woman's Book of Courage*, *The Woman's Book of Confidence*, and *Freedoms after Fifty*. She lives with her husband, Gene, near their children and grand-children, in Colorado.

TO OUR READERS

Conari Press, an imprint of Red Wheel/Weiser, publishes books on topics ranging from spirituality, personal growth, and relationships to women's issues, parenting, and social issues. Our mission is to publish quality books that will make a difference in people's lives—how we feel about ourselves and how we relate to one another. We value integrity, compassion, and receptivity, both in the books we publish and in the way we do business.

Our readers are our most important resource, and we value your input, suggestions, and ideas about what you would like to see published. Please feel free to contact us, to request our latest book catalog, or to be added to our mailing list.

Conari Press
An imprint of Red Wheel/Weiser, LLC
P.O. Box 612
York Beach, ME 03910-0612
www.conari.com

Email

nKonrade@Mail
Stormx Vail
.org